Empowering Couples:
Building on Your Strengths

Empowering Couples:
Building on Your Strengths

David H. Olson
Amy K. Olson

Life Innovations, Inc.
Minneapolis, Minnesota

Empowering Couples: Building on Your Strengths

Published by Life Innovations, Inc. in Minneapolis, Minnesota

Second Edition

Cover and graphic design: Robyn Lingen

Library of Congress Cataloging-in-Publication Data
Olson, David H. 1940–
Olson, Amy K. 1969–
   Empowering couples: Building on your strengths
            p.   cm.
   Includes bibliographic references

   ISBN 0-9671983-2-1 (softcover only)

   1. Marriage 2. Communication 3. Couples

   Library of Congress Card: 99-091737

Ordering Information:
   Life Innovations, Inc.
   P.O. Box 190
   Minneapolis, MN 55440

   (800) 331-1661

   www.lifeinnovations.com

This book is dedicated to
Karen Olson

My loving partner—David
My mother, my friend—Amy

Contents

Acknowledgements

This book was created with the help of many hearts and hands.

We are very fortunate for the father-daughter collaboration we have. We feel privileged to work together where emotional support and laughter abounds.

We deeply thank Karen who has been the backbone of this and many other projects. Her love, wisdom and belief are our strength.

To the 21,501 married couples who took ENRICH in 1998-1999; without whom the research would not be possible.

Sincere thanks to Sharlene Fye for the help in creating the national sample, and for endless data analysis.

To Luke Knutson, whose contributions are greatly appreciated.

Thanks and gratitude to staff at Life Innovations for editing of the early drafts.

Thanks to Thomas Briggs and Lonnie Bell for valuable copy editing.

To Dr. Rob Gilbert whose friendship and insight are deeply felt and appreciated.

To our families and friends, who are there for us in all the important ways that count.

And to our readers: Many thanks for your interest in creating stronger relationships!

Preface

Congratulations! You have already demonstrated a crucial component to building a stronger and more satisfying relationship—desire and interest. By opening this book, you have overcome one obstacle that prevents many couples from moving their relationship to the next level. By choosing to read *Empowering Couples,* you have decided to equip yourself with some of the tools needed to build a strong and lasting relationship.

No one is foolish enough to build a house without plans, tools, and at least some expertise. But few of us build our relationships with the same care. *Empowering Couples* provides a solid foundation of information, support, and exercises to empower—to build, improve, and energize—your couple relationship.

Foundation of the Book

Empowering Couples is based on over twenty years of research on couples in the PREPARE/ENRICH Program, one of the most popular programs for couples in the world. More than 45,000 counselors and clergy of all denominations have used this program with more than a million couples in the United States. It has been introduced and used in eleven other countries—Australia, Canada, England, Germany, Hong Kong, Japan, Korea, Singapore, South Africa, Sweden and Taiwan.

In the PREPARE/ENRICH Program, couples take one of four couple inventories (PREPARE, PREPARE—MC, ENRICH or MATE) that is relevant to their relationship.

Each inventory contains 195 questions that focus on twenty of the most important areas of a couple's relationship. For this book, we've highlighted several of the most important areas for building strong marriages.

In *Empowering Couples,* we want you to learn what happy couples are doing and what their strengths are. This research is in contrast to most studies which focus on only the problems. In order to empower couples, we feel that emphasizing strong marriages and analyzing differences between happy and unhappy marriages is critical.

Our research sample is 21,501 married couples from fifty states who took the ENRICH couple inventory in 1998 and 1999. From this large sample we looked in depth at 5,153 couples where both partners were happily married and 5,127 couples where both partners were not happily married. Details on the sample and our analysis can be found in the Appendix.

Format of the Book

Each chapter begins with a "couple quiz" about a specific relational topic. Each quiz contains five items that have been found to be important components of couple happiness in the specific area that the chapter addresses. The purpose of the quiz is to personalize the information and enable you to process it in a meaningful way that is focused on your relationship needs. By taking the quiz with your partner, you will get a lot of information about the unique nature of your relationship.

However, each quiz also has individual scoring procedures enabling you to obtain some insight into your relationship even if your partner is not taking the quiz. At the end of each chapter are couples exercises, which build on the couple quizzes and focus on components found to be important for happy marriages.

This is a book you can read alone or with your partner. The exercises are designed so you can take them alone, but the ultimate goal is that you both take the quizzes so you can discuss them together. The book is organized so that chapters build on one another, but it is not necessary for you to read the chapters in the order they are presented.

Goals of the Book

This book will help you do five basic things:

1. Identify your couple strengths.
2. Build and increase your couple strengths.
3. Identify some of your stumbling blocks (issues, problems).
4. Learn how to overcome your stumbling blocks by "Turning stumbling blocks into stepping stones."
5. Empower your relationship by developing a plan for building a stronger and more satisfying couple relationship.

Through examples, reading, and personal application of couples exercises, you can learn and grow, both individually and as a couple.

You will learn the important lesson of how to:

Turn Your Stumbling Blocks into Stepping Stones!

Chapter One

The Path of the Strong

The block of granite, which is an obstacle on the path of the weak,
becomes a stepping stone on the path of the strong.

—Thomas Carlyle (1795–1881)

The only difference between stumbling blocks and stepping-stones is how we choose to use them. In other words, something that we perceive as an obstacle in our life can be overcome by simply changing the way we look at and use it.

A guiding theme of this book is how to turn your stumbling blocks into stepping-stones. The first step is to identify your strengths as a couple. The next step in this process is to identify the issues in your couple relationship that cause the relationship to "stumble"—to lose some of it's original vitality and energy.

In this book, you will have the opportunity to take several Couple Quizzes relating to different aspects of your relationship. The purpose of these quizzes is to bring about couple and self-awareness, which will empower you to examine your thoughts and actions. The quizzes are designed to stimulate conversation between you and your partner, as you discover both your strengths and weaknesses as a couple. After identifying issues that may be obstacles to your relationship growth, you will learn about some tools to overcome them. Our goal is to help you to turn your stumbling blocks into stepping-stones.

Marriage—A Complex System

For one human being to love another is perhaps the most difficult task
of all, the epitome, the ultimate cost. It is that striving for which
all other striving is merely preparation.

—Rainier Maria Rilke (1876–1926)

Marriage can be the most nourishing and most enduring of human relationships. Ironically, marriage can also be the most disappointing, frustrating and conflicted of human relationships. The poet Javan eloquently summarizes this paradox:

We are all born into this World with certain abilities and various needs. The challenge of Life is for us to discover those abilities and to use them, while fulfilling our needs. Our abilities are as many and as varied as there are people, but we will find that our needs are common to all. The need that offers the greatest potential for joy is also the need that offers the greatest potential for pain, the need to share our life with someone.

—Javan, 1984, p.3

Given these extremes in emotions, marriage can be a source of great joy and deep pain as well as a unique combination of strength and vulnerability. Within marriage, individuals have a source of happiness and a haven from the rest of the world. But marriage can also affect partners negatively, making them feel as if they need a retreat from their marriage.

The emotional climate of marriage is only part of its complexity. Marriage is not an isolated system. A multitude of factors affect and are affected by marriage including society, work, family, religion, and friendships, as well as the backgrounds, habits and personalities of each individual.

The Decline of Marriage

In recent decades, several trends associated with marriage have emerged. The number of marriages in our society has decreased since 1970 from 68% of the population marrying to 56% (U.S. Bureau of the Census, 1998). A second trend is an increase in the number of people who never marry or who get divorced and choose not to remarry.

The number of people who have never been married increased from 21 million (16%) in 1970 to 45 million (23%) in 1996. The number of divorced people in the population since 1970 has tripled from 3% to 10% as of 1996. A third trend is an increase in the number of cohabiting couples. In 1970, only 500,000 couples were living together; the number rose to 3.7 million in 1996 and to over 4 million in 1998.

Although most individuals choose to marry at least once, apparently fewer are choosing to remarry and instead either stay single or choose cohabitation over marriage. In sum, marriage has been on the decline for three decades, and there is no evidence to suggest a reversal anytime soon.

The Value of Marriage

Although the popularity of marriage seems to be decreasing, marriage has many positive societal, familial, and personal benefits. Married people tend to be healthier, live longer, have more wealth and economic assets, and have more satisfying sexual relationships than single or cohabiting individuals. In addition, children generally do better emotionally and academically when they are raised in two-parent families (Waite, 1995, 1998; Waite & Gallagher, 1999). Let's look at these benefits in more detail:

MARRIED PEOPLE HAVE A HEALTHIER LIFESTYLE. *People who are married tend to avoid more harmful behaviors than do single, divorced, or widowed persons. For example, married people have much lower levels of problem drinking, which is associated with accidents, interpersonal conflict, and depression. In general, married people lead a healthier lifestyle in terms of eating, exercising, and avoiding harmful behaviors.*

MARRIED PEOPLE LIVE LONGER. *Married people live several years longer than do single, divorced, or widowed persons. This is often because they have the emotional support of their partner and access to more economic resources.*

MARRIED PEOPLE HAVE A SATISFYING SEXUAL RELATIONSHIP. *Over half (54%) of married males and 43% of married females are extremely satisfied with their sexual relationship. For cohabiting couples, about 44% of the males and 35% of females are extremely satisfied.*

MARRIED PEOPLE HAVE MORE WEALTH AND ECONOMIC ASSETS. *Because married couples can pool their economic resources, they tend to be wealthier. In fact, the median household wealth for a married couple is $132,000, as compared to $35,000 for singles, $42,275 for widowed individuals, and $33,670 for divorced individuals.*

CHILDREN GENERALLY DO BETTER IN A TWO-PARENT HOME. *Children from two-parent homes tend to do better emotionally and academically. As teenagers, they are half as likely to drop out of school; they have higher grades; and they are less likely to get pregnant. Children from two-parent homes also receive more parental attention (such as supervision, help with schoolwork, and quality time together) than do children from single-parent homes. In fact, children from single-parent homes have a much higher probability of growing up in poverty and experiencing a lower quality of life.*

Why Love Is Not Enough

"Love is all you need." "Love makes the world go round." "Love means never having to say you're sorry." So much has been written about love that there almost seems to be an overemphasis on and overempowerment of it in our society. Although love is indeed a powerful emotion, it is idealistic to think that love is all you need. Love alone is not enough to make a marriage work. How do we know this? Most Americans report being in love at the time of marriage, yet the divorce rate still continues to be about 50%.

In addition, in many married couples, one person is much happier than their partner. This is demonstrated by the low correlation in marital satisfaction between spouses (r = .56). This correlation means that if you know the satisfaction level of one marriage partner, you will only be able to predict the partner's marital satisfaction 25% of the time.

Studies also indicate that many unhappy couples stay married. In examining different marriage types, Fowers and Olson (1993) found that couples who have a more traditional marriage (strong religious views, traditional role allocation, and high agreement in children and parenting and religion) were less happily married than any other marriage type yet were *least* likely to divorce.

Love is important, but love alone is not sufficient to maintain a healthy, vitalized, and happy marital relationship. Relationship skills, particularly communication and conflict resolution skills, are necessary, as is a strong commitment from both individuals.

Every relationship is unique in terms of what each partner contributes and what synergy is created by the combination of the two personalities. To illustrate this, think about bread. Each of the ingredients used to make bread—flour, yeast, salt, water—is unique, yet very different from the bread that results from combining them. Like bread and relationships, the sum is greater than the parts. That is why it is virtually impossible to make predictions about relationships even when they are based on knowledge of some of the components involved.

Relationships are too complex to make generalized inferences beyond predictions based on majority. Therefore, you are the expert on your own relationship. This book will guide you in assessing your relationship, will teach principles of healthy relationships, and will relate common couple problems and differences between happily married and unhappily married couples.

Stumbling Blocks for Couples

Understanding common relationship problems will help you to realize you are not alone. However, unless you are a professional therapist, you are unlikely to hear about the problems that couples face and must work through in their relationship. It is much more common for couples to share with others only the positive aspects of their lives together.

To identify the most common problematic issues for couples, we conducted a survey of 21,501 married couples. This analysis was done with a national sample to determine both the most problematic relationship areas and the most problematic specific issues.

The top ten specific issues for married couples come from six relationship areas: conflict resolution (3 items); couple flexibility (2 items); personality issues (2 items); communication, leisure activities, and parenting. The high percentage of couples reporting these problems clearly shows the prevalence of specific relationship issues (See Table 1.1).

The specific issue that creates the most problems for couples involves leadership (93%). This is because either the partners disagree with each other about whether leadership is shared equally or they both agree to having an unequal relationship in terms of leadership.

The importance of conflict resolution is indicated by the fact that three of the top ten specific issues that are problematic for couples are from that area. The three specific issues are: "I always end up feeling responsible for the problem" (81%); "I go out of my way to avoid conflict with my partner" (79%); and, "Our differences never seem to get resolved" (78%).

The second most common couple problem is in the area of personality. Specifically, 87% of couples feel their partner is sometimes too stubborn and 83% report that their partner is too negative or critical.

Table 1.1 Top Ten Stumbling Blocks for Couples

ISSUE/PROBLEM	PERCENTAGE OF COUPLES HAVING PROBLEM
1. We have problems sharing leadership equally.	93%
2. My partner is sometimes too stubborn.	87
3. Having children reduces our marital satisfaction.	84
4. My partner is too negative or critical.	83
5. I wish my partner had more time and energy for recreation with me.	82
6. I wish my partner were more willing to share feelings.	82
7. I always end up feeling responsible for the problem.	81
8. I go out of my way to avoid conflict with my partner.	79
9. We have difficulty completing tasks or projects.	79
10. Our differences never seem to get resolved.	78

Couple flexibility is also an important area that has not been revealed in past studies to be problematic for couples. Flexibility is reflected in the most problematic issue where "We have problems sharing leadership equally" (93%). Another problematic issue is that "We have difficulty completing tasks or projects" (79%).

Happy versus Unhappy Couples

Learn from the mistakes of others,
you won't live long enough to make them all yourself.

—Anonymous

One of the reasons for highlighting differences between happy and unhappy couples relates to the quote above. That is, we don't need to make all the mistakes ourselves—we can learn a lot from the experiences of others.

The second set of data from our national survey of married couples involves the characteristics that distinguish "happy" from "unhappy" couples. Based on their scores on a marital satisfaction scale, couples were classified as either "happily married" or "unhappily married." There were 5,153 happily married couples and 5,127 unhappily married couples. The middle group was excluded because either their marital satisfaction scores were both moderate, or one partner was high and one was low. For more details about the sample and analysis, see Appendix A.

Through in-depth analysis using a marital inventory called "ENRICH," we found distinct differences between happily married and unhappily married couples. The ten categories from ENRICH that discriminated the best between happy and unhappy couples were in rank order: communication, couple flexibility, couple closeness, personality compatibility, conflict resolution, sexual relationship, leisure activities, family and friends, financial management and spiritual beliefs.

Table 1.2 rank orders the best items from these ten areas that discriminate between happy and unhappy couples. What this means is that we have identified in rank order the ten most important categories and items for describing happy couples. It was possible to predict with 93% accuracy whether a specific couple was happy or unhappy using these items.

Table 1.2 Top Ten Strengths of Happy Couples

	HAPPY COUPLES PCA*	UNHAPPY COUPLES PCA*
1. I am very satisfied with how we talk to each other.	90%	15%
2. We are creative in how we handle our differences.	78	15
3. We feel very close to each other.	98	27
4. My partner is seldom too controlling.	78	20
5. When discussing problems, my partner understands my opinions and ideas.	87	19
6. I am completely satisfied with the amount of affection from my partner.	72	28
7. We have a good balance of leisure time spent together and separately.	71	17
8. My partner's friends or family rarely interfere with our relationship.	81	38
9. We agree on how to spend money.	89	41
10. I am satisfied with how we express spiritual values and beliefs	89	36

*PCA = positive couple agreement
†This table lists the one item that best discriminates between happy and unhappy couples from the ten ENRICH categories.

Strengths of Happy Couples

Why is it that some couples seem so happy, regardless of life situations, transitions, or circumstances they may encounter? Are they simply well matched individuals? Are they doing something different from less happy couples? What is their secret?

The most important area distinguishing happy and unhappy couples is *communication*. Communication measures individual's beliefs about and attitudes toward the role of communication in the maintenance of the relationship. Items focus on the level of comfort felt by each partner in sharing important emotions and beliefs, perception of each partner's listening and speaking skills, and perceptions concerning one's own abilities to communicate with the partner. Whereas happy couples have a high level of positive agreement (75%) about the quality of their communication, unhappy couples have low agreement (11%).

The communication item found to be most predictive of happily married couples was whether partners agree that they are satisfied with how they talk to each other. Almost all happily married couples (90%) agree with this statement, whereas only 15% of unhappily married couples do so (See Table 1.2).

The second most important category distinguishing happy and unhappy couples is *couple flexibility*. Couple flexibility reflects the capacity of a couple to change and adapt when necessary. Items focus on leadership issues and the ability to switch responsibilities and change rules. For seventy-five percent of happy couples, couple flexibility is a strength, whereas for only 20% of unhappy couples this is true.

The specific couple flexibility item distinguishing most highly between happily married couples and unhappily married couples is agreement on how differences are handled. Seventy-eight percent of happily married couples agree to being creative in how they handle differences, whereas about half (55%) of unhappy couples agree on this item. (See Table 1.2.)

The third-ranking category, *couple closeness*, assesses the level of emotional closeness experienced between partners and the degree to which they balance separateness and togetherness. Items deal with the extent to which

spouses help each other, spend time together, and express feelings of emo
tional closeness. Not surprisingly, partners in happy couples feel much
closer to one another than do those in unhappy relationships (91% versus
35%). The closeness item which discriminates best between happy and
unhappy couples is agreement on feeling very close to each other (happy
couples 98%; unhappy couples 27%).

Another important difference between happy and unhappy couples
relates to *personality compatibility*. Items focus on issues such as tardiness,
temper, moodiness, stubbornness, jealousy, and possessiveness, as well as
personal behaviors related to public demonstration of affection and the use
of chemical substances. In addition, this subscale considers spouses' general
outlook, dependability, and tendency to be domineering. Happy couples are
much more likely (63%) than unhappy couples (11%) to feel compatible
with their partner's personality. The specific personality item which distinguishes between happy and unhappy couples best is whether the partners
agree that their partner is not too controlling. Happy couples have much
more agreement on this item than unhappy couples do (happy 78%;
unhappy 20%).

The fifth ranking category which distinguishes best between happy and
unhappy couples is *conflict resolution*. Conflict resolution focuses on individuals' attitudes, feelings, and beliefs about the existence and resolution of
conflict in the relationship. Items pertain to the openness of partners in rec-
ognizing and resolving issues, the strategies and processes used to end arguments, and the level of satisfaction with the manner in which problems are
resolved. Most happily married couples (61%) like how they handle conflict,
while only 12% of unhappily married couples do so. Specifically, happily
married couples are much more likely to agree to feeling understood when
discussing problems than unhappily married couples are (happy 87%;
unhappy 19%).

Sexual relationship, Leisure activities, Family and friends, Financial
management and Spiritual beliefs are other major components in distinguishing between happy and unhappy couples. Most happy couples have

high agreement on questions regarding their sexual relationship, (happy 81%; unhappy 26%). A majority of happy couples have high agreement on issues about leisure activities (66% happy; 25% unhappy). Happy couples also have much higher agreement than unhappy couples on issues regarding family and friends (happy 82%; unhappy 40%), financial management (happy 69%; unhappy 25%), and spiritual beliefs (happy 81%; unhappy 46%). Table 1.2 presents the specific items which differentiate best between happy and unhappy couples in these areas. These findings clearly demonstrate that happy couples have significantly more relationship strengths than unhappy couples.

Knowledge Is Power

You can't stop the waves, but you can learn to surf.
—Jon Kabat-Zinn

Simply understanding the differences and obstacles in our relationship removes some of the power they have over us. Awareness generates in us the ability to maneuver more intelligently, perhaps by confronting the challenge that these stumbling blocks pose rather than tripping over them. There are numerous examples in literature of this concept in action, including the following story:

A 10-year-old boy decided to study judo despite the fact that he had lost his left arm in a devastating car accident. The boy began lessons with an old Japanese judo master. The boy was doing well, so he couldn't understand why, after three months of training, the master had taught him only one move. "Sensei," the boy finally said, "shouldn't I be learning more moves?"

"This is the only move you know, but this is the only move you'll ever need to know," the sensei replied. Not quite understanding, but trusting in his teacher, the boy kept training.

Several months later, the sensei took the boy to his first tournament.

Surprising himself, the boy easily won his first two matches. The third match proved to be more difficult, but after some time, his opponent became impatient and charged; the boy deftly used his one move to win the match. Still amazed by his success, the boy was now in the finals.

This time his opponent was bigger, stronger, and more experienced. For a while, the boy appeared to be overmatched. Concerned that the boy might get hurt, the referee called a time-out. He was about to stop the match when the sensei intervened. "No," the sensei insisted, "let him continue."

Soon after the match resumed, his opponent made a critical mistake: He dropped his guard. Instantly, the boy used his move to pin him. The boy had won the match and the tournament. He was a champion.

On the way home, the boy and the sensei reviewed every move in each match. Then the boy summoned the courage to ask what was really on his mind.

"Sensei, how did I win the tournament with only one move?"

"You won for two reasons," the sensei answered. "First, you've almost mastered one of the most difficult throws in all of judo. And second, the only known defense for that move is for your opponent to grab your left arm."

The boy's biggest weakness had become his biggest strength.

—Bits and Pieces (1997)

Turning Your Stumbling Blocks into Stepping Stones

Relationships are dynamic and changing. Many factors can propel your relationship into either positive or negative change, including life cycle stages, time, and events or behaviors within or without the relationship. What is important is the realization that your relationship is dynamic and changing. By reading and working through this book, you can improve your relationship, regardless of the problems you may have.

The good news for couples who have a lot of problems in their relationship is that simply by being willing to take action toward improvement, they will see positive change more rapidly. To illustrate, think about someone who is 100 pounds overweight versus someone who is 15 pounds overweight. Upon implementing diet and lifestyle changes, the person with more weight to lose is bound to see results sooner than the person with less weight to lose. So, instead of becoming discouraged by the perceived problems, see them as opportunities for growth, change, and improvement.

There is a direct relationship between actions and outcome. We control our actions: therefore, we control our lives. A problem in a relationship calls attention to issues that need to be addressed in the same way that illness is your body's way of telling you things like "Rest more," "Relax," or "Take care of yourself." A relationship problem communicates a lot about the needs of the individuals involved. Relationship components such as sex and communication are emotional barometers of other aspects of the relationship.

All of your choices and actions will have some kind of result. Motivational speaker Les Brown said, "If you want to keep on getting what you're getting, keep on doing what you're doing." But if you want to achieve something different, you and your partner both must be willing to do something different. Many couples who want changes make the mistake of using the same approach over and over, and they keep getting the same result. Listen to your partner and your own needs and take new steps to make your partnership more mutually satisfying.

Five Types of Married Couples

One interesting way to assess your couple relationship involves thinking in terms of various types of couples. This may help you to focus on specific aspects of your relationship. A national study of 6,267 married couples identified five distinct types of marriage (Olson & Fowers, 1993). These types are summarized here and graphically depicted in Figure 1.1.

Figure 1.1 Five Types of Married Couples

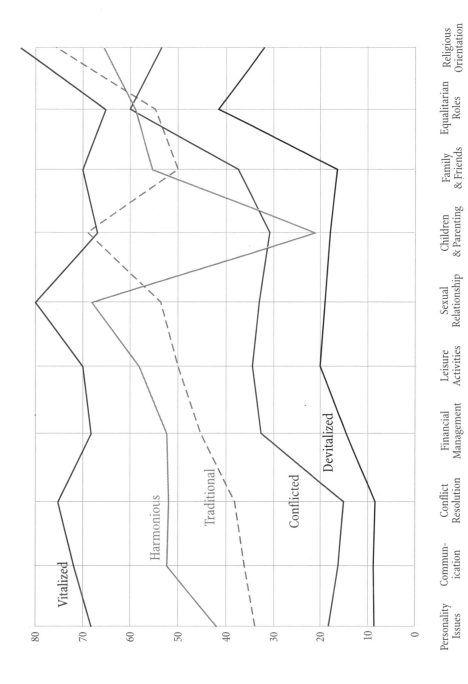

VITALIZED COUPLES. These represent the happiest couple type, as is reflected in the fact that they have the highest couple scores on most aspects of their relationship. Vitalized couples have many strengths, including the conflict resolution, communication, and sexual relationship domains. Only 14 % of individuals in vitalized marriages ever considered divorce.

HARMONIOUS COUPLES. These couples are very happy and have many strengths, but not as many as the vitalized couples. Only 28 % of the individuals in harmonious marriages ever considered divorce. They are satisfied with many areas of their relationship, including the role relationship, communication, and conflict resolution domains. While they tend to have lower scores in the children and parenting domain, this is primarily because many couples have no children, which lowers their scores in this category.

TRADITIONAL COUPLES. These couples are generally happy and are called traditional because they have more strengths in traditional areas, including the children and parenting, family and friends, roles, and religious orientation domain. However, they have lower scores on issues involving more internal dynamics; they indicate problems with the personality issues, communication, and conflict resolution domains. Over one-third (37%) of the traditional couples have considered divorce.

CONFLICTED COUPLES. These couples are unhappy and have numerous growth areas and few relationship strengths. Nearly three-quarters (73%) of the individuals have considered divorce. They are called conflicted since they disagree in many areas and have low scores on the communication and conflict resolution domains as well as many others. Conflicted couples commonly seek marital therapy (Fowers, Montel & Olson, 1996).

DEVITALIZED COUPLES. These couples are very unhappy and have growth areas in almost all aspects of their relationship. In over two-thirds (69%) of the couples, both spouses are dissatisfied, and about 90% of these individuals have considered divorce. They are typically very unhappy and have few strengths as a couple, although they might have had strengths earlier in their relationship.

Conflicted and devitalized couples are the two types that most often seek marital therapy and also couple enrichment programs. A recent study (DeMaria, 1998) found that a majority (93%) of couples attending a couple educational program called PAIRS were either conflicted (34%) or devitalized (59%). Only 7% of the couples enrolled in the PAIRS Program were either vitalized or harmonious.

Four Types of Premarital Couples

Four out of five of the same couple types were identified with a sample of 5,030 premarital couples. As expected, the couple type that was not found in premarital couples was the devitalized type (Fowers & Olson, 1992). In this study, there were 1,279 couples (28%) of the vitalized type, 1,249 couples (27%) of the harmonious type, 1,053 couples (23%) of the traditional type and 1,037 couples (22%) of the conflicted type.

A longitudinal study sought to discover the outcome of couple types on marital success (Fowers, Montel & Olson, 1996). A sample of 328 premarital couples were followed for three years after marriage to find out whether there were any differences in levels of marital success among these four different types of premarital couples. As predicted, vitalized couples represented the highest percentage of happily married couples (60%), followed by harmonious (46%), traditional (34%), and conflicted (17%). One interesting finding is that traditional couples had the highest percentage of less happily married couples (50%) yet were the least likely to be separated or divorced (16%). Many conflicted couples (30%) were also less happily married, followed by harmonious (29%) and vitalized (23%). In terms of divorce, over half (53%) of conflicted couples ended up divorcing, while only 17% of vitalized couples had divorced.

What is Your Couple Type?

How do these findings about couple types apply to your relationship? First, as these couple types demonstrate, there are a variety of marriages in terms of strengths and issues. Second, one of these types might seem somewhat like the type of couple relationship you currently have with your partner. Third, these types can give you ideas about what you might want to change in your relationship. Fourth, consider what specific areas of your relationship you would like to improve and what ultimate type of marriage you might like to have with your partner. So reflect on each of these couple types before you move on to other sections in this book.

Whether you have been together for a few months or for many years as a couple, one purpose of this book is to get you to focus more on your couple strengths. In order to do so, you will first be looking at both strengths and growth areas and then concentrating on building your strengths.

We have found that how much a couple focuses on strengths versus problems changes over time. When individuals are dating or in the earlier stages of their relationship, they naturally think about and notice the things about their partner that they like. And they often overlook negative qualities or regard them as unimportant. Unfortunately, this pattern tends to decline after they have been together for a while. We commonly see married couples doing the opposite—focusing on the negative aspects of their partner and their relationship and not thinking as much about their couple strengths.

Focus is power. What you focus on will tend to gain importance and influence your perceptions. As a child, you may have experienced this phenomenon with a magnifying glass and the sun. Even though the sun is 93 million miles away, by focusing its energy in one area, you can create enough heat to make a fire.

Focus also impacts your couple relationship. If you focus on the positive, you will naturally become more aware of the positive and enable your relationship to grow and thrive. *Our goal is to empower you and your partner to build on your strengths—the things that brought you together and that can help you build a more vital and mutually satisfying relationship.*

In everyone's life…

In everyone's life there are problems to solve,
Even in the strongest relationship,
    there are differences to overcome.

It is easy to give up when confronted with difficulties;
    to fool yourself into believing that
    perfection can be found somewhere else.
But true happiness and a lasting relationship are found
    when you look inside yourself
    for solutions to the problems.

Instead of walking away when things get tough
    and blaming the other person,
    look for compromise and forgiveness.
Caring is not a matter of convenience.
    It is a commitment of one soul to another.

And if each gives generously of themselves,
    then both lives are enriched.
The problems will come and go,
    just like the changing seasons.
But unselfish love is constant and everlasting.

—Susan Staszewski

Chapter Two

Communication— The Key to Intimacy

Talking is the major way we establish, maintain, monitor and adjust our relationships.

—Deborah Tanner

Communication Quiz

How satisfied are you with your communication as a couple?

You can take this Communication Quiz alone and see how you score individually using the format and scoring at the end of the chapter.

Encourage your partner to also take the Communication Quiz so you can identify your strengths and issues regarding communication as a couple. Instructions for scoring and discussing the Quiz are described at the end of the chapter in Couple Exercise 2.2.

Response Choices

1	2	3	4	5
Strongly Disagree	Disagree	Undecided	Agree	Strongly Agree

1. We are good at sharing positive and negative feelings with each other.

2. My partner is very good at listening to me.

3. We let each other know our preferences and ideas.

4. We can easily talk about problems in our relationship.

5. My partner really understands me.

Communication—The Essential Ingredient

The three most important words for a successful relationship
are communication, communication, and communication.

—Anonymous

Developing a relationship without communication is like trying to make orange juice without oranges: it is impossible. Communication is the one crucial ingredient that defines a relationship. Once a relationship is established, however, communication remains the key skill for maintaining intimacy. In fact, the quality of communication becomes more important as the level of intimacy in a relationship increases. We clearly expect our partners to listen with more interest and to speak with more sensitivity than we would expect from an acquaintance we run into while grocery shopping.

Communication is vital and essential because it is the link to every aspect of your relationship. The outcome of discussions and decisions about finances, children, careers, religion, and even the expression of feelings and desires will all depend on the communication styles, patterns, and skills you've developed together.

Communication has the power to bring couples together and the ability to push couples apart. The willingness and ability to communicate contribute greatly to the health and happiness of a couple relationship. The good news is that good communication skills—speaking and listening—are something that can be learned and improved upon, as you will see in this chapter.

Common Stumbling Blocks to Communication

It is a luxury to be understood.

—Ralph Waldo Emerson

Communication and intimacy are closely interrelated. Couples, especially unhappy spouses, are often heard to complain that, "We don't communicate." But it is impossible not to communicate. In fact, the absence of conversation, physical contact, smiles or self-disclosure "communicate" a lot about the feelings people have toward each another. Our national survey of 21,501 married couples identified specific communication issues that are problematic for married couples. (Table 2.1 summarizes the findings).

Table 2.1 Stumbling Blocks regarding Communication

COMMUNICATION ISSUE	PERCENTAGE OF COUPLES HAVING PROBLEM
1. I wish my partner were more willing to share feelings.	82%
2. I have difficulty asking my partner for what I want.	75
3. My partner does not understand how I feel.	72
4. My partner often refuses to discuss issues/problems.	71
5. My partner makes comments that put me down.	67

The majority of married couples (82%) wish that their partners would share feelings more often. Many spouses have difficulty asking their partner for what they want (75%), do not feel understood (72%) and feel that their partner will not discuss issues with them (71%). Still another common problem with married couples is feeling put down by their partner (67%).

Making Assumptions

Assumptions are the termites of relationships.

—Henry Winkler

One pattern couples fall into that may contribute to feelings of being misunderstood is the tendency for spouses to assume they know each other. While couples are dating, the individuals are often asking each other questions and talking about their life experiences. But the longer two people are together, the more they think they know each other and so neglect to ask questions and continue learning about each other.

Although it may be comforting at times to feel understood by your partner without having to explain your feelings, this may eventually lead to communication problems. For example, we often see married partners finishing each other's sentences. This may become problematic when the spouses assume that they know how each other thinks or feels about something and fail to ask or check out an issue.

The assumptions one person makes can be false if they are based on past experiences and presume that the other person has not changed. But people's feelings and ideas often change. Although our bodies may quit growing around the age of 19, the most drastic changes are not physical and are a continuous part of living. Assuming you know your partner's thoughts and feelings can cause you to take each other for granted and lead to a decrease in communication, which results in less sharing and intimacy.

Drifting from Positive to Negative Communication

Engaged couples and couples in the early stages of marriage tend to look for the positive qualities in their partners and either overlook negative qualities or regard them as unimportant. Slowly and subtly, however, this pattern can shift so that partners who have been married for many years tend to be more focused on the negatives in the other person and in the relationship. And according to the survey results in Table 2.1, 67% of couples are unhappy with negative comments from their partner.

Because we tend to see only what we are focused on, the negative focus of couples can create even more problems. For example, have you ever bought a new car and suddenly noticed that a lot of people are driving the same car you are? In reality, there are not more people driving that same model of car, but your focus has changed so that you now notice that car more. We tend to find what we are looking for, what we are focused on. Thus, in your marriage, if you are focused on the negatives and you share with your partner the negatives, you will tend to "see" and come to believe that there are mainly negatives.

John Gottman and his colleagues have conducted longitudinal studies on over 2,000 married couples and found that happy couples on average have five times as many positive interactions and expressions as negative interactions and expressions (Gottman, 1994). Gottman refers to this 5-to-1 ratio as "the magic ratio." What this means is that stable couples do not necessarily have less negativity in their relationship, but the negativity is greatly outweighed by positive feelings and actions. Gottman also points out that anger is harmful only if it is expressed along with criticism.

Dr Herbert H. Clark, a psychologist at John Hopkins University, discovered that it takes the average person about 48 percent longer to understand a sentence using a negative than it does to understand a positive or affirmative sentence. This is confirmation of something every successful person knows: The secret of good communication is positive affirmation.

—Bits and Pieces (1996)

Failing to Listen

We're born with two ears and one mouth.
That ought to tell us something.

—Bits and Pieces (1997)

Comedian Lily Tomlin urges us to "listen with the same intensity reserved only for talking." If one communication skill could be considered paramount for developing and maintaining intimacy, it would be listening. We can hear someone talking but not actually be listening. Good listening skills require patience, as well as the ability to withhold judgment and to spend more energy trying to understand.

In order to relate effectively with anyone, you must learn to listen. This means that you should not be planning your response or deciding whether you agree or disagree; you must simply listen with openness and intensity. This is important because, if you listen while holding firmly to your own perspective, you will inevitably try to fit what you hear into your own paradigm. In that case, what you call agreement with someone is based not on what you currently hear, but on what fits into your pre-existing beliefs. To really listen involves withholding your own beliefs.

Effective listening can also be hindered by listening defensively, which is more common if you feel personally attacked by the speaker. Your own feelings and beliefs are important, but they can get in the way of objective and effective listening. Your inner voice sends you messages based on the speakers content, such as "That hurts," "I'm not letting him get away with this," or "That is wrong." These judgments will interfere with your ability to really understand the speaker.

An important listening skill that minimizes defensiveness and judging is *paraphrasing*. Paraphrasing can be understood as operating at two levels: (1) restatement of the speaker's idea by rephrasing to them, and (2) a description of the speaker's ideas and feelings about the idea. Although this approach to giving feedback slows down communication, it minimizes misunderstanding and conflict. The following example demonstrates the two levels of giving feedback by paraphrasing:

Suzanne: *"I'm really fed up with these kids!"*

Michael (restating the idea—level 1): *"Sounds like the kids are acting out."*

Michael (focusing on feelings—level 2): *"You really seem very frustrated, and it sounds like you need time away from the kids."*

By not only restating the content, but also dealing with the feelings reflected in the statement, the speaker ends up feeling understood and appreciated.

What's Your Communication Style?

There are three common styles of communication in relationships: passive, aggressive and assertive. The healthiest and most effective style is assertiveness. The following description of each communication style can help you identify both your own and your partner's typical style and better understand how to work toward assertive communication together.

Passive Communication

Passive communication is characterized by an unwillingness to honestly share thoughts, feelings, or desires. It may stem from low self-esteem, and it is typically used to avoid hurting others' feelings or to avoid being criticized. Although it may be done with good intentions in mind ("I didn't want to hurt them," or "I was afraid I'd say the 'wrong' thing"), passive communication generally leaves the other person in the relationship feeling angry, confused, and mistrustful. Passive communication is a barrier to true intimacy within relationships.

Aggressive Communication

Aggressive communication is characterized by blaming and accusatory actions and is often accompanied by language like "You always" or "You never." It is generally used when one person in the relationship is feeling threatened or is having negative feelings and thoughts. When people communicate aggressively, they are often trying to hold other people responsible for their own feelings. Aggressive behavior focuses on the negative characteristics of the *person* rather than the *situation*, as we see in the following example. This typically leaves both partners feeling hurt and tears down intimacy between them.

Focus on the person: *"You said you'd get the car tuned up and you didn't. You never do what you say you're going to do."*

Focus on the situation: *"I am disappointed that you didn't get the car tuned up before our trip. I am really worried about the tires and the oil needs changing. Do you have time to run it by the shop this morning?"*

Over time, both passive and aggressive communication styles can be detrimental to a marriage. By working toward more assertive behavior, couples can improve their communication, and thereby enhance their marriage.

Assertive Communication

Assertive communication allows people to express themselves in a healthy, nondefensive, and noninsistent way. It means asking clearly and directly for what one wants, and being positive and respectful in one's communication. An example of an assertive statement would be "I would like you to spend more time with the children. Perhaps you can spend one evening alone with them and I can work late at the office." When one partner speaks assertively, it encourages the receiver of the message to also respond positively and assertively.

Communication Styles and Intimacy

Table 2.2 lists typical communication styles, as well as the associated relationship style, outcome and intimacy level. For example, the passive couple is typified by *not* asking for what they want, and so partners usually will not get what they want. The result is a devitalized relationship with a low level of intimacy. When one partner is aggressive and the other is passive, the aggressive partner tends to dominate the relationship, which also results in low levels of intimacy. And when both partners use an aggressive style, their relationship is likely to be conflicted with low intimacy.

In contrast, assertive communication allows both partners to win, increasing the intimacy of the relationship and keeping it growing and alive. But it is important for both individuals to use assertive communication styles. If one partner is assertive and one is passive, the relationship will become frustrating for both individuals, and they will have low intimacy. If one partner is assertive and one is aggressive, the relationship may be very confrontational, which also results in low intimacy.

Table 2.2 Communication Patterns and Intimacy

Person A COMMUNICATION	Person B	RELATIONSHIP	WHO WINS	LEVEL OF INTIMACY
Passive	Passive	Devitalized	Both lose	Low
Passive	Aggressive	Dominating	I win, You lose	Low
Aggressive	Aggressive	Conflicted	Both lose	Low
Assertive	Passive	Frustrated	Both lose	Low
Assertive	Aggressive	Confrontational	Both lose	Low
Assertive	Assertive	Vital/Growing	Both win	High

Strengths of Happy Couples

Our goal is to identify the path of the strong—learning from couples who are happily married. Experience is undeniably the best teacher. Other people's hindsight can certainly become your foresight. With this principle in mind, let's briefly review the results from our national sample of married couples. To discover the communication issues that distinguish happily married and unhappily married couples we will review the major findings (see Table 2.3).

Spouses in happy couples are six times more likely than those in unhappy couples to agree that they are very satisfied with how they talk to each other. These spouses are significantly more likely to feel understood by their partners, and they find it much easier to express their true feelings than their unhappy counterpoints. A majority of happy spouses believe that their partners are good listeners, whereas only a small percentage of unhappy spouses feel this way. And almost four-fifths of happy spouses agree that they do not make comments to put each other down, compared to only one-fifth of unhappy spouses.

Table 2.3 Strengths of Happy versus Unhappy Couples regarding Communication

| | PERCENTAGE IN AGREEMENT | |
| | HAPPY | UNHAPPY |
COMMUNICATION ISSUE	COUPLES	COUPLES
1. I am very satisfied with how we talk to each other.	90%	15%
2. My partner understands how I feel.	79	13
3. I find it easy to express my true feelings to my partner.	96	30
4. My partner is a very good listener.	83	18
5. My partner does not make comments that put me down.	79	20

Improving Communication with Your Partner

A Conversation a Day

Every living thing needs nurturing and attention. If you wanted to plant a tree and have it thrive, you wouldn't simply set the tree in the yard and hope for the best. Instead, you would dig a hole and carefully place the sapling in it. Then you would fill the hole and fertilize and water the tree. And you would carefully monitor its growth, checking for insects and disease.

It is the same with your couple relationship. Your marriage needs attention on a daily basis, which can be as simple as 5 minutes of meaningful dialogue. The focus of this daily dialogue should be on your feelings about each other and your life together. So, set aside 5 minutes per day and 15 minutes on the weekends to discuss the following:

What you most enjoyed about your relationship that day.
What was dissatisfying about your relationship that day.
How things could be made better for each of you.

Couples typically resist discussing negative feelings because they do not want to create problems or arguments. But what really happens when issues are not discussed is the opposite. As in an untended garden, ignored feelings have a weedlike way of taking over, of growing up through ever-widening cracks. Eventually, they may lead to resentment, disinterest, and a lack of desire to repair the relationship. Spouses who wait too long to discuss things that are bothering them gradually become apathetic toward each other. You must take care of your marriage as you would any living thing if you want it to thrive.

Self-Disclosure

One way to create intimacy in your relationship is through self-disclosure. *Self-disclosure* is the revelation of deeply personal information about yourself, things that most people may not know. By sharing your innermost thoughts and most private experiences, you bring your relationship to a deeper level.

Self-disclosure creates an environment of mutual trust, which benefits both individuals. When you share your thoughts and dreams with someone special, you not only reveal yourself to that person, but also learn about yourself. It feels good to be open, and it also feels good to have someone confide in you.

Self-disclosure has a reciprocal effect as well. When we confide in others, they increasingly will confide in us. Studies show that married couples typically share more negative feelings and fewer positive ones. However, those couples who are most happy in marriage share a lot of both positive and negative feelings (Gottman, 1994). Whereas silence isolates us, self-disclosure connects us.

Assertiveness and "I" Statements

Both happily married and unhappily married couples experience conflict, but happily married couples have learned how to deal with conflict constructively. Two important communication skills used more often by happily married couples are assertiveness and "I" statements.

Assertiveness is the ability to express feelings and ask for what you want. Assertive individuals do not assume that their partners can read their minds; they ask clearly and directly for what they want. Assertiveness allows you to express your rights without infringing on the rights of others. What's more, it works!

An analysis of personality characteristics using the PREPARE/ENRICH couples program showed that people who have high scores on assertiveness also tend to be low in avoidance and partner dominance behaviors. They also like their partner's personality, feel good about their communication and like how they resolve couple conflict.

An *"I" statement* is a statement about your feelings. "I" messages are important because they communicate facts without placing blame and are not likely to promote defensiveness in the receiver. Since "I" messages do not communicate blame, they are more likely to be understood. In contrast, *"You"* messages create defensiveness because they sound accusatory. For example, think about how you would respond to the following "I" and "You" statements:

"You" statement:

"You are so inconsiderate to me in front of your friends!"

"I" statement:

"I feel hurt when you put me down in front of your friends."

Other "you" statements to avoid include "You always…" ("You're always late") and "You never…" ("You never think about anyone except yourself"). "Always" and "never" are one-dimensional accusatory words that cut down the other person, impelling him or her to deny everything you have said. After all, it would be quite unlikely that somebody would *always* or *never* act in a certain way.

Active Listening

> We hear only half of what is said to us, understand only half of that,
> believe only half of that, and remember only half of that.
>
> —Mignon McLaughlin

Active listening is the ability to listen accurately and repeat back to the speaker the message you heard. In active listening, the listener verbally feeds back what he or she hears in order to clarify that the message has been accurately received and interpreted. The following is an example of an assertive statement and an active listening response:

Assertive statement: *"I enjoy spending time with you, but I also want to spend more time with my friends. I would like us to find some time to talk about this."*

Active listening: *"I heard you say that you enjoy the time we spend together but that you need more time to be with your friends. You want to plan a time to talk about this."*

Active listening ensures that both the sender and receiver of a message are clearly understood and that there is little room for misinterpretation.

Daily Compliments

Giving your partner at least one compliment each day may sound simplistic, but it can have a remarkable effect on your relationship. We often are more inclined to compliment acquaintances or co-workers than our spouses. Giving at least one daily compliment to your partner will help you focus on your strengths as individuals. It will also highlight the positive qualities that initially attracted you to each other. Notice in Table 2.3 that only 20% of unhappy spouses feel that their partner does not make comments that put them down. In other words, 80% of unhappy couples feel that their partner puts them down.

Instead of making comments to put your partner down, make compliments to boost them up! Think of the two of you as a team. Supporting your partner personally will inevitably benefit both of you. Daily compliments will prevent your relationship from becoming routine and make it more mutually satisfying. Receiving a compliment not only makes you feel good but also makes you feel good about the person giving the compliment.

Couple Exercise 2.1
Improving Your Communication

Once you and your partner have read the chapter on communication, you can explore the uniqueness of your relationship by doing the following exercises. Complete this exercise separately. You can either photocopy the pages, or write directly in the book.

List three things that you really like about how your partner communicates.

PARTNER 1   PARTNER 2

1. _____   1. _____
2. _____   2. _____
3. _____   3. _____

Now list three things that you would like your partner to change about how he or she communicates.

PARTNER 1   PARTNER 2

1. _____   1. _____
2. _____   2. _____
3. _____   3. _____

After you have completed your individual lists, share and discuss them with each other. Talk about the things you agree to work on changing.

Couple Exercise 2.2
Discussing Your Strengths and
Growth Areas in Communication

TAKING COMMUNICATION QUIZ:

Each partner should take this Communication Quiz and record your responses below.

IDENTIFY YOUR COUPLE STRENGTHS:

Strengths are the items where you both agree with each other. Circle those items. *Strengths = Each of your answers are 4 or 5.*

COUPLE DISCUSSION:
1. Discuss your strengths and be proud of them.
2. Discuss the other items and decide how you can turn them into strengths.

Response Choices

1	2	3	4	5
Strongly Disagree	Disagree	Undecided	Agree	Strongly Agree

	PARTNER 1	PARTNER 2
1. We are good at sharing positive and negative feelings with each other.	_____	_____
2. My partner is very good at listening to me.	_____	_____
3. We let each other know our preferences and ideas.	_____	_____
4. We can easily talk about problems in our relationship.	_____	_____
5. My partner really understands me.	_____	_____

Scoring of the Quiz

1. Individually take the quiz.

2. Score quiz by summing your five answers.

   PARTNER 1:_____   PARTNER 2: _____

3. Interpreting your score: Range = 5–25

   21–25 = Your communication is very good.
   15–20 = Your communication is generally good, but there are some ways
   it could be improved.
   11–14 = Your communication is good in some ways, but also needs
   some improvement.
   5–10 = Your communications needs improvement.

4. After you have both taken and scored the Quiz, compare how you perceive
   your relationship regarding communication.

Suggestions for Improving Your Communication

1. Focus on the good in each other.

2. Praise each other often.

3. Take time to listen. Listen to understand, not to judge. After listening, tell your partner what you heard before you share your own ideas.

4. Be assertive. (Using "I" statements rather than "you" statements) Let your partner know what you want—don't let your needs become a guessing game.

5. Give your relationship the importance and attention you did when you first met.

**Turn your stumbling blocks
into stepping stones!**

Chapter Three

Conflict
Resolution

Happiness is not the absence of conflict, but the ability to cope with it.

Conflict Resolution Quiz

How satisfied are you with your conflict resolution as a couple?

You can take this Conflict Resolution Quiz alone and see how you score individually using the format and scoring at the end of the chapter.

Encourage your partner to also take the Conflict Resolution Quiz so you can identify your strengths and issues regarding conflict resolution as a couple. Instructions for scoring and discussing the Quiz are described at the end of the chapter in Couple Exercise 3.3.

Response Choices				
1	2	3	4	5
Strongly Disagree	Disagree	Undecided	Agree	Strongly Agree

1. We are able to compromise when necessary.

2. We tend to ignore issues that may cause conflict.

3. We often allow minor issues to become major problems.

4. We have different ways of dealing with issues.

5. We are generally able to work through issues and resolve them.

The Problem Isn't the Problem

The way we handle problems, more than the problems themselves, often can be the problem. Conflict is a natural and inevitable part of human relationships. People in a relationship are going to have differences, and relations will not always be harmonious. And as partners become closer, these differences inevitably will cause some disagreements. However, the fact that conflict exists in intimate relationships does not necessarily mean that love is absent. In fact, conflict can be beneficial to a relationship if it is handled and resolved in a healthy way.

How effectively couples deal with anger and conflict is critical to their relationship growth. Without effective conflict resolution skills, a couple's relationship will become stagnant and will decrease in vitality. People need to focus on improving their skills to effectively resolve conflict.

Common Stumbling Blocks to Conflict Resolution

Perceptions of Conflict

When you think of the word conflict, what images come to mind? Are these images positive or negative? The first stumbling block to conflict resolution is probably a faulty perception of conflict itself. If two individuals immediately see conflict as negative, and therefore avoid talking about it, their relationship will suffer.

Conflict is common and it does not have to damage a relationship. Rather, problems arise when couples do not know how to manage conflict. Our national survey of 21,501 married couples identified the top five issues regarding conflict resolution for couples (see Table 3.1). According to the survey, most couples disagree on the issue of who is responsible for a given problem. Many couples feel that their differences never seem to get resolved, and partners will go out of their way to avoid conflict with each other. A majority of couples have different ideas about the best way to solve disagreements and report having serious disputes over trivial matters.

Table 3.1 Top Five Stumbling Blocks regarding Conflict Resolution

Conflict Issue	Percentage of Couples Having Problem
1. One person ends up feeling responsible for the problem.	81%
2. I go out of my way to avoid conflict with my partner.	79
3. Differences never seem to get resolved.	78
4. We have different ideas about the best way to solve disagreements.	78
5. We have serious disputes over unimportant issues.	78

Love and Anger

Anger is a brief madness.
—Horace (658 B.C.)

Just as perceptions about conflict get in the way of empowering your relationship, views of anger also can inhibit intimacy. Keep in mind that, like conflict, anger can be a natural aspect of a close relationship. It may seem strange that we can be polite and considerate to strangers and yet be cruel to our partners whom we love. But the reality is that, relatively speaking, closer relationships offer more opportunities for anger to arise than casual acquaintances do.

Anger is a destructive emotion that only intensifies conflict. But anger is usually a symptom of some issue within the relationship that needs to be addressed and possibly changed. Feelings of anger must be dealt with carefully and deliberately. Sometimes you have to bite your tongue in a moment of anger, backing off until you feel calmer. As the saying goes, *"There are three things that never return: the past, the neglected opportunity and the spoken word."* In a moment of rage, you may say something that can never be taken back and that your partner may never forget.

Once you have separated yourself from the situation and had some time to think through your anger, you will be able to discuss the issue with more clarity. This is important to do. Keep in mind that thinking through anger is very different from suppressing anger. Suppressed anger is dangerous to a relationship because it means that the issue is never resolved. Rather, the issue will simmer beneath the surface, often causing resentment, which can poison the relationship. So, instead of concealing your anger or blowing your stack, be intentional about identifying the source of your feelings and then discuss it calmly with your partner.

Problems Just Don't Go Away with Time

Most couples are afraid of the negative emotions associated with dealing with problems. A common response is to ignore the issue, hoping it will disappear with time. But if a problem is not resolved, it continues to fester, and eventually it may lead to feelings of bitterness or even hatred. In their extensive couples research, Howard Markman and colleagues identify avoidance as one of the key relationship patterns that is predictive of unhappiness and divorce (Markman, Stanley, & Blumberg, 1994).

Just as with any physical illness or mechanical breakdown, the sooner you treat the problem, the easier it will be to cure or fix. For example, if you suddenly developed an acute pain in your chest, you would not ignore it because it might be a symptom of a serious illness. Or if the brakes in your car suddenly screeched loudly every time you hit them, you most likely would take the car in to be repaired. The same is true in your relationships. It is impor-

Figure 3.1 Hierarchy of Conflict Model

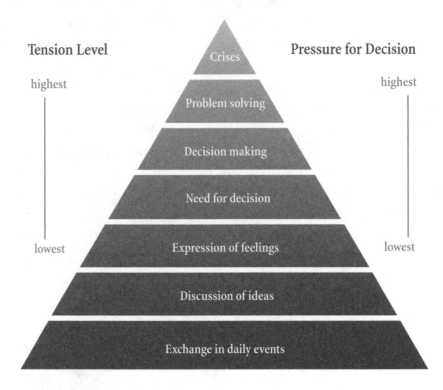

tant not to ignore the warning signs that your relationship needs some attention. Problems almost never go away with time, and they often get worse.

The Hierarchy of Conflict Model illustrates a continuum of dialogue potential ranging from exchanges on daily events to crises (see Figure 3.1). The lowest three levels in the conflict hierarchy represent common reasons that individuals get together to relate: namely, to chat about daily events, to discuss ideas, and to express feelings. These discussions generally operate at a low level of tension, and there is usually little pressure to make any decisions.

The next four levels in the hierarchy involve increased tension levels and need for discussion. An awareness of the need for a decision precedes actual decision making. If a decision that should be made is not made, a problem might develop that would then need to be solved. And if the problem is not solved, it could lead to a crisis, which is even more difficult to resolve.

For example, Greg and Laura are a young couple needing to make some financial/budget decisions. During a recent trip to Las Vegas, they spent much more money than intended; in fact, they spent all their extra spending money. So, when their electric bill came the next month, they did not have enough money to pay it. This represents the "decision-making" phase of the Hierarchy of Conflict Model. Greg and Laura are obviously aware of the problem, and they need to make a decision. Maybe they can ask for help from their parents or friends, or maybe they can drastically cut back on other expenses for the next month in order to pay the bill. Or perhaps they choose to not make a decision at all.

The next level is the "problem solving" phase. Problems can arise for Greg and Laura either because they choose to make no decision or because they make a bad decision. If they choose to not make a decision, then the problem only becomes more serious. For instance, if they don't pay the bill, the next month the bill will be doubled. And if they still don't pay it, the electric company may disconnect their power. At this point, Laura and Greg would be in the "crisis" phase. In order to get their power reconnected, they would have to fall behind on their house mortgage. But now they would be risking foreclosing on their mortgage and losing the money they have invested into their home.

Lack of Conflict Resolution Skills

Many people simply do not have the skills necessary to resolve conflicts effectively. After all, very few of us were fortunate enough to have had a relationship skills course in school. School may have taught us algebra or chemistry, but we had to learn conflict resolution through trial and error. If we were lucky enough to receive good feedback, we may have learned along the way about ineffective ways of dealing with conflict. Two very common ways that people ineffectively deal with conflict are (1) blaming the other person and (2) bringing up old issues.

Blaming Other Person. Blamers spend a lot of time and energy trying to change other people. They essentially try to hold others responsible for their feelings and see others, rather than themselves, as the problem. But remember this saying: "When you point a finger at someone, there are three fingers pointing back at yourself." In other words, a problem is almost never the fault of only one person; all people involved contribute in some way to the issue.

Feeling anger and assigning blame can become an ineffective and endless cycle. Other people do not cause your problems or serve as the source of your unhappiness. And since the only person you can change and control is yourself, you might as well use the energy wasted on blaming someone to clarify your own thoughts, feelings, and preferences. Ask yourself, "What is the real issue here?" and "What do I want to change?" By focusing on what you desire from the relationship and how that can be achieved, you can learn to use anger effectively.

Bringing Up Old Issues. Couples research tells us that happily married partners engage in discussions about conflict in nondestructive ways (Olson, 1996). One common but destructive way of dealing with anger and conflict involves bringing up old issues in your relationship. Dredging up past hurts only leads to increased feelings of anger, pain, and defensiveness. And when you feel you have to defend yourself, you are not able to negotiate and solve the real issue at hand. Stay in the present. It is the only place where things are really happening.

CATHY© Cathy Guisenite. Reprinted with permission of UNIVERSAL
PRESS SYNDICATE. All rights reserved.

Differing Conflict Resolution Styles

Regardless of the issue, most partners tend to repeat the same patterns when they argue. Harriet Goldhor Lerner (1985) developed a guide to styles of anger management, labeling these styles pursuer, distancer, overfunctioner, underfunctioner, and blamer.

PURSUERS seek to create connections so they can become more intimate and close. Because talking and expressing feelings is important to them, they tend to feel rejected by their partner if the partner wants more space. When the partner or important person in their life withdraws, pursuers will tend to pursue more intensely.

DISTANCERS tend to be emotionally distant. They have difficulty showing vulnerability and dependency. They often manage stress by retreating into their work and may terminate a relationship when things become too intense. They are less likely to open up emotionally when they feel they are being pursued.

UNDERFUNCTIONERS typically have several areas in their lives in which they just can't seem to get organized. They tend to become even less organized when under stress. They have difficulty displaying their strong and competent side in intimate relationships.

OVERFUNCTIONERS are quick to advise and help out when others are having problems. They seem to know what's best for others as well as for themselves, so they are often labeled as "reliable." They often have difficulty showing their vulnerable, underfunctioning side.

BLAMERS tend to react to stress with emotional intensity and combative behavior. They like to try to change others and to put others down in order to make themselves look good.

Couples often fall into patterns of dealing with conflict that do not change. Regardless of what they argue about, they will tend to follow the same pattern. In Couple Exercises 3.2, you and your partner can assess your conflict resolution styles. Gaining an awareness of the style each person typically uses is part of the process of developing more constructive ways of resolving issues.

Strengths of Happy Couples

Table 3.2 summarizes the key differences between happy and unhappy couples. The most significant item that distinguished happy and unhappy couples in our national survey of 21,501 married couples as they deal with conflict is whether the partners feel understood when discussing problems. Individuals in happy couples are much more likely than those in unhappy couples to feel understood by their partners and to feel able to share feelings and opinions during disagreements. Happy couples are also much more likely to agree that their disagreements get resolved than unhappy couples are. Finally, partners in happy couples are much more likely to agree that they have similar ideas about how to resolve conflicts and to take disagreements seriously.

Table 3.2 Strengths of Happy vs. Unhappy Couples regarding Conflict Resolution

| | PERCENTAGE IN AGREEMENT | |
| | HAPPY | UNHAPPY |
RELATIONSHIP ISSUE	COUPLES	COUPLES
1. When we discuss problems, my partner understands my opinions and ideas.	87%	19%
2. I can share feelings and ideas with my partner during disagreements.	85	22
3. We are able to resolve our differences.	71	11
4. We have similar ideas about how to settle disagreements.	64	13
5. My partner takes our disagreements seriously.	78	26

Constructive and Destructive Approaches to Conflict Resolution

Peace cannot be kept by force. It can only be achieved by understanding.
—Albert Einstein (1879-1955)

Choosing the Right Approach

During times of conflict, does your partner understand you? If so, it is likely that you are both using constructive conflict resolution skills. If not, you may have to change your approach. The good news is that conflict management is a skill that anyone can acquire.

Many components of conflict resolution allow for different approaches, and the approaches used will dramatically affect the outcome and the feelings of the partners involved. Some approaches are constructive while others are destructive. Let's examine both.

In destructive approaches to conflict resolution, old issues are often brought up. In constructive conflict resolution, the focus is solely on the relevant and current issues. When partners argue destructively, they tend to express only negative feelings; in constructive conflict resolution, they share both positive and negative feelings. Destructive quarrelers often share only select information with each other as they try to hold the other partner responsible.

Constructive conflict resolution involves not pointing fingers of blame but sharing the facts of the situation, even if they do not always support an individual's contention. Further, the fact that both people involved contribute to the problem is emphasized. Destructive conflict resolution resists change, while constructive approaches encourage change in order to develop new ways of handling problems. And, perhaps most noteworthy, the level of emotional closeness decreases when couples engage in destructive conflict resolution; the result of constructive conflict resolution is often increased intimacy and trust in the relationship.

Table 3.3 compares the various components of the constructive and destructive approaches, as well as the outcome of each. Because the approach you use to resolve conflict will affect the outcome, the more constructive your approach, the greater the possibility of success.

Dealing with Issues and Events

In the book *Fighting for Your Marriage* (1994), Markman and his colleagues discuss the connection of issues and events and the importance of dealing with them separately. Although couples report that major issues in their relationship cause problems (money, communication), they tend to argue frequently about everyday annoyances. This is because, unless they

Table 3.3 Constructive and Destructive Approaches to Conflict Resolution

AREA OF CONCERN	
Constructive Approach	**Destructive Approach**
ISSUES	
Raises and clarifies issues	Brings up old issues
FEELINGS	
Expresses both positive and negative feelings	Expresses only negative feelings
INFORMATION	
Gives complete and honest information	Offers only select information
FOCUS	
Concentrates on the issue rather than the person	Concentrates on the person rather than the issue
BLAME	
Accepts mutual blame	Blames the other person for the problem
PERCEPTION	
Focuses on similarities	Focuses on differences
CHANGE	
Facilitates change to prevent stagnation	Minimizes change, increasing conflict
OUTCOME	
Recognizes that both win	Fails to recognize that one wins and one loses, or both lose
INTIMACY	
Increases intimacy by resolving conflict	Decreases intimacy by escalating conflict
ATTITUDE	
Builds trust	Creates suspicion

deal constructively with the major issues, related events can easily trigger an angry outburst. These events represent the overall feelings about and attitude toward the bigger picture—the major issues. Dealing with issues rather than events releases some of the power that these issues contain.

A very simple example could be housework. If partners do not share the same expectations for the division of housework and do not work through a solution together, the potential for conflict will remain below the surface, ready to be triggered by an event. Suppose Sarah and Robert have been married for a year. In Sarah's family, housework was divided among family members, while Robert came from a more traditional family in which the mother did most of the housework. During their first year of marriage, Sarah took on the responsibility for the housework. In Sarah's opinion, it simply needed to get done, and because Robert wasn't doing it, she did it.

Lately, however, Sarah has started to resent having to do everything herself. Her work schedule has demanded more of her time, and she finds herself spending her free time cleaning bathrooms and shopping for groceries while Robert plays golf and watches TV. Yet Sarah has not said anything to Robert about her feelings, and he is unaware that there is a problem. One Saturday afternoon, Sarah is putting clothes away when Robert returns from playing golf with friends. Tired and frustrated, Sarah explodes, yelling at Robert about his golf. To Robert, it may seem that Sarah is making too big a deal about his playing golf, but the real issue involves housework, which is not discussed. The biggest mistake Sarah and Robert can make is to not discuss the issue of housework outside of this event. What is bound to happen then is that a similar event will eventually trigger another argument. They need to sit down and talk about their feelings and discuss solutions.

Ten Steps for Resolving Couple Conflict

The goal in marriage is not to think alike, but to think together.
—Robert C. Dodds

When you have issues that are ongoing or recurring, use this ten-step approach to deal with them. Couple Exercise 3.1 may boost your ability to deal with issues that resist resolution. Focus on one issue at a time, and allow yourselves at least 30 minutes to complete the exercise.

The following is an example of how a married couple, Gary and Melissa, used the ten-step procedure to work through an issue.

1. Set a time and place for discussion. Gary and Melissa set aside 30 minutes on Saturday afternoon at 2 o'clock to share and discuss, focusing on this one specific issue.

2. Define the problem or issue of disagreement. The issue they have chosen is a complaint of Gary's, but it has caused tension in their relationship several times before. Gary is upset because he feels that Melissa makes decisions without asking his opinion.

3. Talk about how each of you contributes to the problem. Melissa admits to making plans without asking for Gary's input. Gary concedes that he is often indecisive and that Melissa is a better decision maker. Still, Gary often feels as if he has little control over how they spend time as a couple.

4. List past attempts to resolve the issue that were unsuccessful. In the past, Melissa has made all the plans because Gary is slow to act on them. Gary tries to give input, but it is difficult for him to do that.

5. Brainstorm ten new ways to resolve the conflict. For instance, Melissa will not make major decisions without consulting Gary. Gary will try to be more assertive in expressing his preferences. They will not make a rush decision. Each night after dinner, Melissa and Gary will discuss upcoming plans. They will check and recheck with each other about plans. Neither Melissa nor Gary will make any new plans for the next week.

6. Discuss and evaluate these possible solutions. Melissa and Gary talk about each solution and share with each other what they like and dislike about each one.

7. Agree on one solution to try. Melissa and Gary decide to start discussing upcoming plans with each other every night after dinner.

8. Agree on how each of you will work toward this solution. Melissa agrees to not make any plans without consulting Gary, and Gary agrees to practice being assertive by asking about the plans at dinner.

9. Set up another meeting to discuss your progress. Melissa and Gary decide to meet again next Saturday at 2 o'clock to discuss how they feel the plan is working.

10. Reward each other as you each contribute toward the solution. Melissa and Gary plan to treat themselves to dinner at their favorite restaurant as a reward for their efforts toward resolving this issue.

Couple Exercise 3.1
Ten-Step Procedure for Resolving Conflict

Use the ten-step model when there is a problem that comes up frequently that you have not been able to resolve. Try it with your partner now. Start with a minor ongoing issue in your relationship.

In step 5, brainstorm at least ten new ways to resolve the issue. Do not judge ideas based on whether they are feasible. Simply come up with as many ideas as possible, even if they may seem far-fetched. Brainstorming in this way will allow you to get beyond what you have done in the past that has not worked.

1. Set a time and place for discussion.

_____

2. Define the problem or issue of disagreement.

_____

_____

3. Talk about how each of you contributes to the problem.

_____

_____

_____

4. List past attempts to resolve the issues that were not successful.

_____

_____

_____

5. Brainstorm ten new ways to resolve the conflict.

a. _____ f. _____

b. _____ g. _____

c. _____ h. _____

d. _____ i. _____

e. _____ j. _____

6. Discuss and evaluate these possible solutions.

_____

_____

_____

_____

7. Agree on one solution to try.

_____

_____

_____

8. Agree on how each of you will work toward this solution.

_____

_____

_____

_____

9. Set up another meeting to discuss your progress.

_____

10. Reward each other as you each contribute toward the solution.

_____

_____

_____

Couple Exercise 3.2
Identifying Your Conflict Resolution Styles

Complete the following scale to discover your conflict resolution styles. Rate yourself and your partner on each conflict resolution style. Write an "S" where you think your own style falls and a "P" to represent your partner's.

PARTNER 1: Refer to page 52 for descriptions of styles.

Pursuer	0__1__2__3__4__5__6__7__8__9__10__
Distancer	0__1__2__3__4__5__6__7__8__9__10__
Underfunctioner	0__1__2__3__4__5__6__7__8__9__10__
Overfunctioner	0__1__2__3__4__5__6__7__8__9__10__
Blamer	0__1__2__3__4__5__6__7__8__9__10__

PARTNER 2: Refer to page 52 for descriptions of styles.

Pursuer	0__1__2__3__4__5__6__7__8__9__10__
Distancer	0__1__2__3__4__5__6__7__8__9__10__
Underfunctioner	0__1__2__3__4__5__6__7__8__9__10__
Overfunctioner	0__1__2__3__4__5__6__7__8__9__10__
Blamer	0__1__2__3__4__5__6__7__8__9__10__

Discuss with your partner any discrepancies in the style you think you use and the style he or she perceives you to use.

Couple Exercise 3.3
Discussing Your Strengths and Growth Areas in Conflict Resolution

TAKING CONFLICT RESOLUTION QUIZ:
Each partner should take this Conflict Resolution Quiz and record your responses below.

IDENTIFY YOUR COUPLE STRENGTHS:
Strengths are the items where you both agree with each other. On items 1 and 5, circle those items if you both agreed (response 4 or 5). On items 2, 3, and 4, circle those items if you both disagree (response 1 or 2). *Circle the Strength items you identified.*

COUPLE DISCUSSION:
1. Discuss your Strengths and be proud of them.
2. Discuss the other items and decide how you can turn them into strengths.

Response Choices

1	2	3	4	5
Strongly Disagree	Disagree	Undecided	Agree	Strongly Agree

	PARTNER 1	PARTNER 2
1. We are able to compromise when necessary.	_____	_____
2. We tend to ignore issues that may cause conflict.	_____	_____
3. We often allow minor issues to become major problems.	_____	_____
4. We have different ways of dealing with issues.	_____	_____
5. We are generally able to work through issues and resolve them.	_____	_____

Scoring of the Quiz

1. Individually take the quiz.

2. Score the quiz as follows:
     a. Total your points for items 1 and 5.   _____
     b. Add 18 to total of a.   __+ 18__
     c. Total points for items 2, 3, and 4.   _____
     d. Subtract c from b.   _____

   PARTNER 1:_____   PARTNER 2: _____

3. Interpreting your score: Range = 5–25

     21–25 = Your conflict resolution is very good.
     15–20 = Your conflict resolution is generally good, but there are some
             ways it could be improved.
     11–14 = Your conflict resolution is good in some ways but also needs
             some improvement.
      5–10 = Your conflict resolution needs improvement.

4. After you have both taken and scored the Quiz, compare how you perceive
   your relationship regarding conflict resolution.

Suggestions for Improving Your Ability to Resolve Conflict

1. View conflict as a normal part of a close relationship.

2. Never negotiate in moments of anger. Take some time to compose yourself so that you will be able to rationally discuss the issue.

3. When negotiating, do not bring up past issues.

4. Do not blame each other, but focus on the problem. Remember that everyone involved contributes in some way.

5. Deal directly with issues as they arise. If an issue keeps coming up, use the ten-step model to work through it.

**Turn your stumbling blocks
into stepping stones!**

Chapter Four

Role
Relationships

*Throughout history the more complex activities have been
defined and redefined, now as male, now as female,
sometimes as drawing equally on the gifts of both sexes.
When an activity to which each sex could have contributed
is limited to one sex, a rich, differentiated quality
is lost from the activity itself.*

—Margaret Mead (1901–1978)

Role Relationship Quiz

How satisfied are you with your role relationship as a couple?

You can take this Role Relationship Quiz alone and see how you score individually using the format and scoring at the end of the chapter.

Encourage your partner to also take the Role Relationship Quiz so you can identify your strengths and issues regarding how you handle roles as a couple. Instructions for scoring and discussing the Quiz are described at the end of the chapter in Couple Exercise 4.3.

Response Choices

1	2	3	4	5
Strongly Disagree	Disagree	Undecided	Agree	Strongly Agree

1. A career can be equally important to a man or a woman.

2. To maintain an equalitarian relationship, we need to negotiate and compromise more often.

3. If both partners are working, the husband should do the same amount of household chores as the wife.

4. We divide our household chores based on interests and skills rather than on traditional roles.

5. We make most decisions jointly.

Sharing Roles: Making It Fair

Coming together is easy; keeping together is progress;
working together is success.

—Henry Ford (1863–1947)

Roles relate to how couples handle leadership responsibilities and divide household tasks. In a traditional relationship, the woman is primarily responsible for taking care of the household and children, the man's career generally takes precedence over the woman's, and decision making is more often the man's responsibility. In egalitarian relationships, partners share considerably more of the household, child-care, and decision-making responsibilities.

The definition of roles as male or female is constructed by society and reflects who wields social power. In our society, traditional male characteristics, such as aggression and logic, are more valued than traditional female characteristics, such as sensitivity and understanding. These values are reinforced through the society we live in, but their social status has nothing to do with their actual worth.

While most young couples, especially women, prefer the idea of a more equalitarian relationship, this is harder to achieve than you might think. It takes more relationship skills to develop and maintain an equalitarian relationship because there are more things to negotiate. Who does the laundry? Who pays the bills? Who does the shopping? Who takes care of the cars? Who cleans? Especially after children arrive, the woman often becomes more involved in child-care and housework than the man, and the couple relationship becomes even less equalitarian.

Roles—Common Stumbling Blocks

Women are made, not born.

—Simone de Beauvoir (1908–1986)

Couples actually can and do create the roles of husband and wife. But many subtle and overt factors affect how roles become established, including societal expectations, childhood experiences, and individual preferences and experiences.

Tradition

Historically, women played the role of housekeeper, laundress, chauffeur, cook, errand runner, nanny, dishwasher, dietitian, gardener, tutor, and so on. In many families, girls were expected to help with housework more than boys were. The role models that our families provide for us are powerful agents in shaping behavior.

Individual preferences in roles often get overlooked when roles are established. Unfortunately, most couples fall into roles without ever actually discussing their preferences and wishes. Many couples try to dismiss roles and household responsibilities as trivial matters that do not threaten their relationship, the truth is that roles profoundly influence the quality of the relationship. Although roles may seem trivial, the sheer amount of time that they demand can make them larger than life. In addition, the consequences of how roles are divided are not trivial. In researching 600 couples filing for divorce, George Levinger found that "neglect of home and children" was second only to "mental cruelty" as the reason cited for divorce (Thorton, 1997). Relationship roles also tell a lot about the power dynamics in the relationship and are a symbol of relationship equality.

Table 4.1 lists the top five role issues based on our national survey of 21,501 married couples. The role relationship issue that is most problematic for couples involves the division of household tasks. Many couples also have problems regarding whether the division of household chores is based on interests and skills or on traditional roles. Another common area of disagreement concerns the willingness of the husband and the wife to adjust to the roles. Many couples differ in their opinion of how hard partners work to maintain an equalitarian relationship. Couples also commonly have issues regarding the wife being primarily responsible for running the household even if she also works outside the home.

Table 4.1 Top Five Stumbling Blocks regarding Roles

Role Issue	Percentage of Couples Having Problem
1. Concern about unfair division of housework.	49%
2. Housework is based on traditional roles versus interests.	44
3. The husband is not willing to adjust as much as the wife.	44
4. Woman responsible for running the household in addition to working outside the home.	44
5. Disagree that both work to maintain an equalitarian relationship.	40

Marital Satisfaction and Role Relationship

When it comes to traditional roles and the happiness and vitality of a marriage, it appears that the "good old days" may not have been so good after all. As Table 4.2 shows, married couple's perceived role relationship is significantly related to the partners' marital satisfaction. Like the comparison we did in previous chapters, happy and unhappy couples were compared. This time the focus was on the type of role relationship they each had established.

A clear finding was that couples who perceive their relationship as traditional in terms of roles are much more likely to be unhappy than couples who perceive their relationship as equalitarian. If both people perceive their relationship as traditional, more than four-fifths of them are unhappy with their marriage, while less than one-fifth are happy. Similarly, when both people perceive their relationship as equalitarian, more than four-fifths have a happy marriage, while less than one-fifth are unhappy.

Table 4.2 Role Relationships in Happy Versus Unhappy Couples

	Percentage in Agreement		
	HAPPY COUPLES	UNHAPPY COUPLES	TOTAL
Perception of Relationship	(n=5,153)	(n=5,127)	(n = 10,280)
Both perceive as equalitarian	81%	19	100% (n = 4,130)
Husband perceives as traditional, wife perceives as equalitarian	50	50	100% (n = 1,267)
Wife perceives as traditional, husband perceives as equalitarian	37	63	100% (n = 1,561)
Both perceive as traditional	18	82	100% (n = 3,322)

For couples in which the woman perceives the relationship as traditional and the male views it as equalitarian, almost two-thirds are unhappy while only about one-third are happy. If the husband perceives the relationship as traditional and the wife perceives it as equalitarian, an equal percentage of the couples are happy and unhappy. So, the more equal they both perceive the role relationship, the happier they are in their marriage.

Unequal Distribution of the Dirty Work

The American male's life cycle resembles something out of zoology—
a juvenile phase during which we are cared for by our mothers;
a short free-swimming interlude where we semicare for ourselves;
and a mature phase where we once again resume
our place being cared for by females we love.

—James Thorton

If you were to look only at housework as a sign of the times, you might be fooled into thinking we still live in the 1950s. Arlie Hochschild's 1989 book, *The Second Shift* coined a phrase that a lot of women can relate to. Many women are returning home from their jobs only to be faced with their second job of maintaining the household and raising the children.

Women clearly have been the recipients of an unfair division of labor in the home. In fact, in only 20% of dual-career marriages in Hochschild's study did the men share housework equally with their wives. This adds up to a lot of extra work for the average woman. Over the course of one year, a woman will work an extra month of 24-hour days just on household tasks (Thorton, 1997).

One study found that single mothers spend an average of 16 hours per week on chores while married mothers spend an average of 20 per week (Thorton, 1997). This has caused some researchers to conclude that, for many husbands, their major contribution toward the household is to create more mess. Women who "do it all" tend to suffer from chronic exhaustion, have a low sex drive, and get sick more frequently. The result is that both partners forfeit their health, happiness, and often the vitality of their marriage.

Reality versus Ideal in Household Tasks

Although attitudes and expectations are changing, women still bear almost all of the responsibility for housework. Even if a husband believes he should share responsibility for cooking, doing the laundry, and shopping for groceries, shared responsibility is more of an ideal than a reality. Women who work full-time still often do the majority of housework.

In a recent survey of 555 randomly selected married people by James Sexton (Thorton, 1997), men claimed to do an adequate share of domestic chores, but most women countered their claims by saying their husbands did very little at home. Two-thirds of the women reported doing most, if not all, of the housework while only 13% of the men reported doing that much housework. Conversely, almost 45% of the men said they did 25% or less of the housework while only 9% of the women reported doing that little housework.

Not only do women do a majority of the housework, but men are significantly less involved in all aspects of housework. As Table 4.3 shows, 84-93% of women reported doing common household tasks such as vacuuming and cleaning the toilet in the past week. For these same tasks, only 46-60% of men reported doing them in the past week.

Table 4.3 Gender Differences in Completing Common Household Tasks

HOUSEHOLD TASK	IN PAST WEEK		HUSBAND NEVER HAS	
	WOMEN	MEN	WOMEN	MEN
Clean toilet	89%	46%	59%	17%
Vacuum house	84	60	27	7
Change sheets	93	57	53	15
Clean refrigerator	86	54	68	24

Source: Thorton, 1997

There are also considerable differences in what husbands and wives each report. (See Table 4.3.) Apparently, men are overreporting their involvement and women are underreporting their husbands' involvement. For example, 59% of the women reported that their husband has never cleaned the toilet while only 17% of men reported that they never cleaned the toilet. Twenty-seven percent of women said that their husbands never vacuumed the house, but only 7% of husbands agreed. A majority (68%) of wives reported that their husbands never cleaned the refrigerator while only 24% of husbands agreed. And 53% of wives say that their husbands never have changed sheets, but only 15% of husbands reported the same.

Unequal Power

All animals are equal, but some animals are more equal than others.

—George Orwell

One issue closely related to role allocation is power. Power can be a major impediment to the achievement of marital equality. According to one classic model, power in a relationship can be divided in four basic ways: (1) a *husband-dominated* power pattern, in which the man is basically the boss; (2) a *wife-dominated* power pattern, in which the woman is basically the boss; (3) an *egalitarian* power pattern, in which authority is shared and decisions are made on a joint basis in most areas; and (4) an *autonomic* power pattern, in which each spouse has about equal authority but in different areas of life, so they essentially make decisions in their particular domains independent of each other. These patterns are illustrated in Figure 4.1.

Janice Steil and Beth Turetsky (1987) studied 815 dual-career couples to investigate the relationship between marital power and psychological well-being. They found that patterns of power in marriage are closely related to individual and couple well-being. For example, marriages based on equality are correlated with greater relationship satisfaction, more sincere and shared types of influence, less depression (particularly for women) and increased intimacy for both partners.

Figure 4.1 Four Types of Leadership

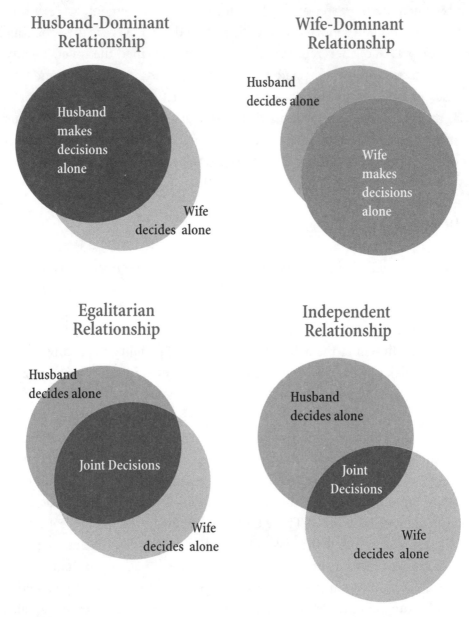

Egalitarian: shared authority and joint decision making in most areas

Independent: about equal authority, but in different areas of life

In contrast, inequality effects both partners negatively. Inequality for the more powerful partner results in less relationship satisfaction, sincerity, and intimacy. For the partner with less power, consequences include low self-esteem, depression, dependency, and hostility toward the other partner.

Marital satisfaction and intimacy are much more likely when partners share responsibilities and decision making. Having a choice about who performs what tasks is also an important aspect of marital satisfaction. Partners who have an egalitarian power pattern tend to be more involved and happier with each other. They are less likely to assign blame because they accept more responsibility for each other's happiness. They also tend to make better decisions because their decisions are based on the wisdom and perspective of two people.

Marriage often reproduces the power patterns partners witnessed as children, which may make relating to each other equally more difficult. In this case, partners may need to work harder on communicating positively and achieving a fair and equal partnership. In the past, most marriages were traditional, and it was hard to conceptualize an equal marriage because it was not modeled in life.

Women's Contribution to the Problem

Women have convinced ourselves that we can do what men can do.
But we haven't convinced ourselves, and therefore we haven't
convinced our country, that men can do what women can do.

—Gloria Steinem

Women's roles have expanded considerably in recent decades while husband's roles have remained quite stable. A majority (56%) of mothers with children are employed, and women make up almost half of the workforce. Yet women still assume a disproportionate responsibility for the work of relationships, the home, and children.

Women typically act as facilitators of change in relationships, yet this inequality in the home has changed very little over the past 30 years. Why? In some cases, women may be sending mixed messages to men. Although they may be exhausted from and irritated by excessive responsibilities, they do not want to give up the control they have in the home. Women may have a hard time surrendering some of their responsibilities to their husbands because so much of their identity is tied to home and children, just as a man's identity is stereotypically tied to his work. Therefore, many men find that when they try to do their share of housekeeping and child care, they are critiqued and judged by their wives to the point of feeling discouraged.

Strengths of Happy Couples regarding Roles

Happy couples have a much more balanced relationship in terms of roles than do unhappy couples. This claim is clearly supported by an analysis of 10,280 married couples whose ENRICH scores on the marriage satisfaction scale were related to scores on individual Role Relationship items; Table 4.4 summarizes the results. Two role issues are particularly related to whether the couple is happily married. The first is the couple's agreement that the husband is as willing to adjust in marriage as the wife. For example, in a traditional role relationship, the wife would most often be the one to change her schedule around their child's activities or appointments. In equalitarian relationships, both the husband and wife would make adjustments.

Table 4.4 How Happy versus Unhappy Couples View Their Roles

ROLE ISSUE	PERCENTAGE IN AGREEMENT	
	HAPPY COUPLES	UNHAPPY COUPLES
1. Both are equally willing to make adjustments in their marriage.	87%	46%
2. Both are satisfied with the division of housework.	81	41
3. Both work hard to have an equal relationship.	90	54
4. Couples make most decisions jointly.	89	57
5. Household tasks are divided based on preferences, not tradition.	71	55

Division of household tasks is the second issue that is strongly related to couple satisfaction. Happy couples are much more likely to not feel concerned that one partner is doing more than his or her share of household tasks than unhappy couples are. Another important indicator of a happy marriage is whether both husband and wife work to maintain an equal relationship. Happy couples are much more likely than unhappy couples to agree that both partners work at having an equal relationship. Happy couples also tend to make decisions jointly and to allocate household chores based on interests and skills rather than traditional roles.

Suggestions for Improving Role Relationship

Forget About "Helping"

When it comes to household tasks, erase from your mind the idea of "lending a hand." Helping someone out implies that the job is that person's responsibility in the first place. In his humorous and useful book, *Chore Wars*, Jim Thorton addresses this point nicely:

> *If there is one word that makes working women cringe, it's probably this one: Help. As in "Let me help with the chores, honey." To most of us fellows, such a comment merely epitomizes our nice-guy, decent natures. But to many women, what they really hear is this: "We both know these chores are your ultimate responsibility, dear, but if you spell out exactly what you want me to do, I will begrudgingly help you with your work. And, by the way, you better show me some appreciation for my help. And if you want me to help again, you will have to remind me each and every single occasion this obnoxious task comes up."*

Remember: your marriage is a partnership. Having balance and fairness in terms of household chores clearly benefits your relationship. You also have a good opportunity to positively impact your relationship and your child(ren) by modeling equality.

Discuss Roles Weekly

Many roles are played out in and maintained by daily routines. In order to keep the right balance, you and your partner need to routinely discuss your roles. Remember that roles can be changed. Do what you like to do around the house, do what you're good at, and do what you and your partner have negotiated together as a fair division of labor.

Be Flexible and Open to Change

It is important for couples to work as a team and help each other out. There is considerable evidence that couples with more equalitarian relationships tend to have happier marriages. The more partners are able to share leadership and decision-making tasks, the happier they are. The following story humorously illustrates the overload that many women feel:

> Mary was married to a male chauvinist. They both worked full-time, but he never did anything around the house and certainly not any housework. That, he declared, was woman's work.
>
> But one evening Mary arrived home from work to find the children bathed, a load of wash in the washing machine and another folded and put away, dinner on the stove, and a beautifully set table, complete with flowers.
>
> She was astonished, and she immediately wanted to know what was going on. It turned out that Charlie, her husband, had read a magazine article that suggested working wives would be more romantically inclined if they weren't so tired from having to do all the housework in addition to holding down a full-time job.
>
> The next day, she couldn't wait to tell her friends in the office.
>
> "How did it work out?" one of them asked.
>
> "Well, it was a great dinner." Mary said. "Charlie even cleaned up, helped the kids with their homework, folded the laundry, and put everything away."
>
> "But what about afterward?" her friends wanted to know.
>
> "It didn't work out," Mary said. "Charlie was too tired."
>
> —Bits and Pieces (1994)

Couple Exercise 4.1
Household Tasks: His and Hers

1. List some things you do around the house and some things your partner does around the house. (for example; planning meals, doing yard work, cleaning, caring for a child, or scheduling appointments). Your partner should also separately create the same two lists.

THINGS YOU DO
AROUND THE HOUSE

THINGS YOUR PARTNER
DOES AROUND THE HOUSE

1. _____

2. _____

3. _____

4. _____

5. _____

6. _____

7. _____

8. _____

9. _____

10. _____

1. _____

2. _____

3. _____

4. _____

5. _____

6. _____

7. _____

8. _____

9. _____

10. _____

2. After you have each completed your lists, compare and discuss them. Focus on what you each would like to change about who handles what household tasks.

3. Revise your current lists, finalizing an agreement about tasks that you will each do next week. Set a time to review the new lists.

Couple Exercise 4.2
Switching Roles for Week

First, we encourage you and your partner to complete Couple Exercise 4.1.

Then, as an exercise in role reversal, switch roles with your spouse for a full week. You must discuss each task with each other and describe the specific steps needed to make it work.

At the end of each day, discuss how successful it was and how it felt for each of you.

Couples Exercise 4.3
Discussing Your Strengths and Growth Areas in Roles

TAKING ROLE RELATIONSHIP QUIZ:
   Each partner should take this Roles Quiz and record your responses below.

IDENTIFY YOUR COUPLE STRENGTHS:
   Strengths are the items where you both agree with each other. On items 1 to 5, circle those items if you both agreed (response 4 or 5). *Circle the Strength items you identified.*

COUPLE DISCUSSION:
   1. Discuss your Strengths and be proud of them.
   2. Discuss the other items and decide how you can turn them into strengths.

Response Choices

1	2	3	4	5
Strongly Disagree	Disagree	Undecided	Agree	Strongly Agree

	PARTNER 1	PARTNER 2
1. A career can be equally important to a man or a woman.	_____	_____
2. To maintain an equalitarian relationship, we need to negotiate and compromise more often.	_____	_____
3. If both partners are working, the husband should do the same amount of household chores as the wife.	_____	_____
4. We divide our household chores based on interests and skills rather than on traditional roles.	_____	_____
5. We make most decisions jointly.	_____	_____

Scoring of the Quiz

1. Individually take the quiz.

2. Score quiz by summing your five answers.

   PARTNER 1:_____   PARTNER 2: _____

3. Interpreting score: Range = 5–25

   21–25 = You have a very equalitarian relationship.
   15–20 = Your relationship is generally equalitarian.
   11–14 = You have a transitional relationship—somewhat equalitarian and somewhat traditional.
   5–10 = You tend to have a more traditional relationship.

4. After you have both taken and scored the Quiz, compare how you perceive your relationship regarding roles.

Suggestions for Improving the Quality of Your Role Relationship

1. Remove gender from housework. Talk about and divide housework based on interests and skills rather than on gender.

2. Work to develop and maintain an equal relationship in terms of power and decision making.

3. Keep an ongoing discussion of your expectations and feelings regarding roles and changes you would like.

4. Working together on tasks as a team works best for most couples.

5. Be flexible and be open to change.

**Turn your stumbling blocks
into stepping stones!**

Chapter Five

Managing Finances

To some people, money means power; to others, love.
For some, the topic is boorish, in bad taste.
For others, it's more private than sex.
Add family dynamics to the mix,
and for many you have the subject from hell.

—Karen S. Peterson (1992)

Managing Finances Quiz

How satisfied are you with the way you manage finances as a couple?

You can take this Managing Finances Quiz alone and see how you score individually using the format and scoring at the end of the chapter.

Encourage your partner to also take the Managing Finances Quiz so you can identify your strengths and issues regarding managing finances as a couple. Instructions for scoring and discussing the Quiz are described at the end of the chapter in Couple Exercise 5.4.

Response Choices

1	2	3	4	5
Strongly Disagree	Disagree	Undecided	Agree	Strongly Agree

1. We tend to agree on how to spend our money.

2. I wish my partner were more careful in spending money.

3. I am concerned about our debts and lack of savings.

4. Use of credit cards is a problem for us.

5. It is easy for us to decide how to handle our finances.

The Price of Money

If you sometimes feel as though financial issues dominate your life, you are not alone. It is estimated that we spend up to 80% of our waking hours earning money, spending money, or thinking about money. A survey conducted by American Express Financial Advisors revealed that 66% of Americans spend more time thinking about money and careers than they do about sex, health, or relationships.

What's more, financial issues are the most common source of stress for couples and families. Historically, economics was an important reason for marriage, whereas today finances are a common contributor to divorce. In a classic study of 500 divorced people, Stan Albrecht (1979) identified financial problems as the fourth most common reason cited for divorce. In a recent study that examined couples' problems as reported to marital therapists, 43% of couples reported that money management was a frequent problem in their marriage (Whisman, Dixon, & Johnson, 1998).

No one is immune to problems or potential problems related to money. No matter how much money families have, they always seem to need more. Family therapists point out, however, that many of these arguments are not really about money. Arguments about money may reflect an inability to develop an open and well-organized couple or family system. These arguments also may represent conflict over power and control in the couple relationship, over differing styles of spending and saving, and over different visions of what money can and cannot do, as well as the myriad of personal feelings that money invokes for each individual.

Common Stumbling Blocks to Managing Finances

Home life ceases to be free and beautiful
as soon as it is founded on borrowing and debt.

—Henrik Ibsen (1828–1906)

Couples have trouble dealing with money issues for a number of reasons, as our national survey of 21,501 married couples reveals (See Table 5.1). Many problems occur when one partner thinks the other should be more careful about spending. Although the current trend to marry later in life benefits these couples on many levels, they may have more adjusting to do when it comes to merging partners' finances. Prior to marriage at an older age, individuals are accustomed to making money decisions without having to consider another person.

Table 5.1 Top Five Stumbling Blocks regarding Finances

FINANCIAL ISSUE	PERCENTAGE OF COUPLES HAVING PROBLEM
1. I wish my partner was more careful in spending money.	72%
2. We have trouble saving money.	72
3. We have problems deciding what is more important to purchase.	66
4. Major debts are a problem for us.	56
5. My partner tries to control the money.	51

Having trouble saving money also is a problem for a majority of married couples. Many couples report disagreeing on what is most important to spend their money. Major debts are an issue for over half of married couples, and many couples have disagreements over who should control the money they have.

Different Styles of Spending and Saving

Not surprisingly, saving/spending problems are common among couples because individuals often have different personal styles of spending and saving. Most partners do not find out until after marriage how different their spending/saving styles are. The greater the difference in styles, the greater the possibility of conflict over money.

To better understand the different styles, it helps to visualize a continuum of saving and spending. On one end of the continuum are people who seem to throw money around. These spenders love to spend money on themselves or on others. On the other end are people who compulsively save money. These savers may feel anxious about spending money or worry that there won't be enough.

Most people are somewhere in the middle of the continuum and are able to successfully balance their impulses to spend money with their need to save and budget. However, people also tend to lean toward being either a spender or a saver. It is these tendencies that can cause trouble or lead to disagreements with their partner.

Different Views of the Meaning of Money

Money is not the most important thing in the world.
Love is. Fortunately, I love money.

—Jackie Mason

Money is not simply the paper, coin, or plastic used to buy things. It can be a source of status, security, enjoyment, or control. If partners have incompatible attitudes about money, purchases are more likely to cause conflict between them. Miriam Arond and Samuel Pauker (1987) have identified four common orientations toward money:

MONEY AS STATUS. A person with a status orientation toward money is interested in money as power—as a means of keeping ahead of his or her peers.

MONEY AS SECURITY. A person with a security orientation is conservative in spending and focuses on saving.

MONEY AS ENJOYMENT. A person with an enjoyment orientation gets satisfaction from spending, both on others and on himself or herself.

MONEY AS CONTROL. A person with a control orientation sees money as a way of maintaining control over her or his life and independence from a partner or other family members.

It is possible for a person to have more than one orientation, but not two conflicting approaches—for example, enjoyment and security. A questionnaire for assessing your money orientation is provided in Couple Exercises 5.1.

Overuse of Credit and Credit Cards

Credit card: What you use to buy what you can't afford tomorrow while you're still paying for it yesterday.

Overspending is another common stumbling block, one that often is caused from buying on credit. Although buying on credit is very convenient, credit cards make it easy to overspend and get into debt. Once in the hole, it is a long climb out. The high interest rates on credit card balances (often double or more the rate on bank loans) can make it difficult for many people to pay back more than the interest and finance charges on their debt. Paying the minimum fee each month may seem easier than paying cash for purchases, but you ultimately end up paying much more for that purchase because of the accumulating interest rates.

Lack of Savings or a Saving Plan

Beware of little expenses,
a small leak will sink a great ship.

—Benjamin Franklin (1706–1790)

To figure out how you are doing in terms of saving, figure out your average annual income and then multiply that by the number of years you have been working. Do not worry about being perfectly accurate; simply estimate the total amount of money that you have earned over your lifetime. Now, how much of this amount have you saved? Look at your savings account balance. If you are like most people, it is probably a very minute percentage of the money that has passed through your hands. And most families are not much different from you. After taxes and monthly bills, most families have very little money to save or invest.

Some people are simply unaware of the benefits of saving. Others make the mistake of thinking of saving as merely another demand on their paycheck. Fortunately, it does not take a lot of money to benefit from compounded interest. And savings are important for creating financial security and being prepared for financial crisis such as illness, job loss, pregnancy, or accidents. Table 5.2 shows how compounding interest allows a little bit of money to grow to substantial sums. Time is on your side when it comes to saving for the future.

Table 5.2 If you save $1 a day:
($1/day for 30 days = $30 month)

YEARS	5%	10%
10	$ 4,677	$ 6,195
20	12,381	22,968
30	25,071	68,379
40	45,969	191,301
50	80,391	524,061
60	137,085	1,424,856
70	230,460	3,863,340

Financial Strengths of Happy Couples

In general, even happy couples disagree more about finances than any other topic. However, our national survey of 21,501 married couples revealed clear differences between happy and unhappy couples regarding money issues; Table 5.3 summarizes our findings. Happy couples agree on how to handle money significantly more than do unhappy couples. They also have fewer concerns about debts and the proper amount to save. Clearly, one way to improve your couple relationship is to discuss and agree on relevant financial matters.

Table 5.3 Strengths of Happy versus Unhappy Couples regarding Finances

| | PERCENTAGE IN AGREEMENT | |
| | HAPPY | UNHAPPY |
FINANCIAL ISSUE	COUPLES	COUPLES
1. We agree on how to spend money.	89%	41%
2. I have no concerns over how my partner handles money.	80	32
3. We are satisfied with our decisions about saving.	73	29
4. Major debts are not a problem.	76	35
5. Making financial decisions is not difficult.	80	32

Recognition of the Limitations of Money

There is nothing wrong with men possessing riches.
The wrong comes when riches possess men.

—Billy Graham

Many problems people have with money may be socially induced. Unfortunately, in our culture, we tend to define success in financial terms. As a result, many people are engaged in an endless endeavor to accumulate more money, falsely assuming that money will bring them happiness or fulfillment. These people miss the silver lining because they're waiting for, hoping for, or striving for gold.

It is important to take a look at your financial goals and realistically discern what money can and cannot do for you. The following list reinforces the fact that money cannot buy the most meaningful things that life has to offer.

What Money Can Buy	What Money Can't Buy
A house	A home
A bed	Sleep
Books	Brains
Food	An appetite
Luxury	Culture
Finery	Beauty
Medicine	Health
Flattery	Respect
Companions	Friends
Amusements	Happiness

Joint Financial Decision Making

Although it is true that the best things in life are not things, financial problems and problems within families are often related. After all, it is hard to enjoy life when you are worried about paying the bills.

This is not to suggest that couples need to be rich to be happy. Rather, the issue is one of management. In looking at Table 5.3, notice that happy couples have significantly less financial issues than do unhappy couples, and most of the issues have to do with how financial decisions are made.

Research shows that couples in which partners feel they have equal control over how money is spent are more satisfied with their relationship than couples in which one partner tends to control money matters. Happily married couples also report a greater influence by the wife and less dominance by the husband in the handling of family finances.

How does a couple gain control over and manage its money? The answer is in budgeting.

Adherence to a Budget

Budgeting gives couples control over their money, rather than having their bills and spending control their lives. Budgeting does not mean cutting back on the things you really want; rather, it is a way to actively decide what you do with your money. It is a conscious, systematic balancing of income and expenses. Or, as one sage put it, it is a way of telling money where you want it to go instead of wondering where it went.

Initially, setting a budget takes some time, but you will find it is time well spent. Developing and living within a budget can keep you out of financial trouble, as well as decrease stress in your couple relationship.

One good way to create a budget is to keep track of everything you spend money on in a given month. You may be surprised at what you spend money on once you put it down on paper.

Sticking to a budget can be difficult at first. You may need to eliminate impulse buying and really practice being disciplined with your money. Allowing a fixed amount each month for items such as gifts and entertainment makes the experience more pleasurable. Having a definite figure in mind helps you avoid spending more than you can afford. And it is a great feeling to know that you are in control of your money.

Plan for Savings

In creating a budget, you and your partner will have an opportunity to decide how much of your income to save. If you find it difficult to save money, you may want to consider having it taken out of your paycheck as an automatic payroll deduction.

Remember, it is never too late or too early to start saving. And money invested in a safe place at a good interest rate continues to grow at a steady rate. Refer to Table 5.2 again to see the results of saving only $30 per month at 5% and 10% interest over time.

Thrift used to be a basic American virtue.
Now the American virtue is to spend money.
—David Brinkley

Couple Exercise 5.1
Money: What Does It Mean to You?

Use the following scale to respond to each of the items below:

Response Choices

1	2	3	4	5
Strongly Disagree	Disagree	Undecided	Agree	Strongly Agree

_____ 1. It is important to me to maintain a lifestyle similar to or better than that of my peers.

_____ 2. In making a major purchase, an important consideration is what others will think of my choice.

_____ 3. Since money equals power, I am willing to work hard for money in order to have more power.

_____ 4. I really enjoy shopping and having nice things.

_____ 5. Saving money for a rainy day is an important principle to live by.

_____ 6. If I had a moderate amount of money to invest, I would be more likely to put it into multiple resources that are relatively safe than into one fairly risky source that has the potential to make a lot of money.

_____ 7. Being "flat broke" is one of the worst things that could happen to me.

_____ 8. Saving for retirement is an important financial goal for me.

_____ 9. If I suddenly came into a windfall of $51,000, I would use the money for something I have always wanted to do or have.

_____ 10. Since "You can't take it with you," you might as well spend it.

_____ 11. Money can't buy happiness, but it sure helps.

_____ 12. Great things in life give me greater pleasure than making a great buy.

_____ 13. I like/would like having my own business because I can/could control my financial destiny.

_____ 14. I like being able to make decisions about how to spend the money I earn.

_____ 15. It bothers me to be dependent on someone else for money.

_____ 16. I feel uncomfortable if someone offers to "pick up the tab" at a meal we have shared because I feel indebted to them.

SCORING AND INTERPRETATION: After taking the quiz, add up your answers to the four questions for each category and record your scores below. Scores for each category can range from 4 to 20, with a high score indicating more agreement with that approach. It is possible to have high or low scores in more than one category. General guidelines for interpreting your scores appear in the box below. Record the interpretation for your score in each category on the scoring chart.

CATEGORY	ADD ITEMS	YOUR SCORE	INTERPRETATION OF SCORE	SCORE	INTERPRETATION
Money as status	1–4	_____	_____	**17–20**	**Very high**
Money as security	5–8	_____	_____	**13–16**	**High**
Money as enjoyment	9-12	_____	_____	**9–12**	**Moderate**
Money as control	13–16	_____	_____	**4–8**	**Low**

Couple Exercise 5.2
Creating a Budget

INCOME

    Partner 1: .... _____

    Partner 2:..................... _____

TOTAL INCOME: .... _____

EXPENSES (monthly)

Housing

    Rent or mortgage: .... _____

    Utilities: .... _____

    Phone:........................ _____

Loans

    Car: .... _____

    House: .... _____

    Personal: .... _____

Transportation

    Gasoline:..................... _____

    Repairs: .... _____

Food

    Food at home:................. _____

    Food away from home: .... _____

Health care: .... _____

Insurance

    Car:.......................... _____

    Home: .... _____

    Life: .... _____

Apparel: .... _____

Personal goods: .... _____

Household supplies: .... _____

Services

    Dry cleaning: .... _____

    Lawn care: .... _____

Other expenditures:

    Charitable contributions: .... _____

    Daycare: .... _____

    Child support: .... _____

    Savings:...................... _____

    Other: .... _____

TOTAL EXPENSES: .... _____

    Surplus or Deficit: .... _____

Couple Exercise 5.3
Setting Short-Term and Long-Term Goals

Goals are dreams with deadlines.
—Diana Scharf Hunt

Individually identify your short- and long-term financial goals. Goals should be realistic and attainable. Once you and your partner have each determined three short-term and three long-term financial goals, share your goals with one another. Decide together how you can reach these goals.

For example, one goal might be to open a savings account to help with your child (or grandchild's) college tuition. Another goal might be to buy a new home. You can then decide exactly how much money you are willing to contribute to this fund every month.

SHORT-TERM FINANCIAL GOALS:

PARTNER 1   PARTNER 2

1. _____   1. _____

2. _____   2. _____

3. _____   3. _____

LONG-TERM FINANCIAL GOALS:

PARTNER 1   PARTNER 2

1. _____   1. _____

2. _____   2. _____

3. _____   3. _____

Couple Exercise 5.4
Discussing Your Strengths and Growth Areas in Finances

TAKING MANAGING FINANCES QUIZ:
Each partner should take this Finances Quiz and record your responses below.

IDENTIFY YOUR COUPLE STRENGTHS:
Strengths are the items where you both agree with each other. On items 1 and 5, circle those items if you both agreed (response 4 or 5). On items 2,3 and 4, circle those items if you both disagreed (response 1 or 2). *Circle the Strength items you identified.*

COUPLE DISCUSSION:
1. Discuss your Strengths and be proud of them.
2. Discuss the other items and decide how you can turn them into strengths.

Response Choices				
1	2	3	4	5
Strongly Disagree	Disagree	Undecided	Agree	Strongly Agree

	PARTNER 1	PARTNER 2
1. We tend to agree on how to spend our money.	_____	_____
2. I wish my partner were more careful in spending money.	_____	_____
3. I am concerned about our debts and lack of savings.	_____	_____
4. Use of credit cards is a problem for us.	_____	_____
5. It is easy for us to decide how to handle our finances.	_____	_____

Scoring of the Quiz

1. Individually take the quiz.

2. Score the quiz as follows:
   a. Total your points for items 1 and 5.   _____
   b. Add 18 to total of a.   ___+ 18___
   c. Total points for items 2, 3, and 4.   _____
   d. Subtract c from b.   _____

   PARTNER 1:_____   PARTNER 2: _____

3. Interpreting your score: Range = 5–25

   21–25 = You handle finances very well.
   15–20 = Your finances are handled well, but there are some ways it could be improved.
   11–14 = Your financial management skills are good in some ways but also need some improvement.
   5–10 = Your financial management skills need improvement.

4. After you have both taken and scored the Quiz, compare how you perceive your relationship regarding financial management.

Suggestions for Improving Your Finances

1. Review and update your financial goals monthly.

2. Talk about what each of you value most in life and whether money relates to those values.

3. Talk about the spender-saver pattern in your relationship.

4. Review any major debt you may have and plan how you will pay them off.

5. If you have ongoing financial problems, seek the help of a financial advisor.

**Turn your stumbling blocks
into stepping stones!**

Chapter Six

Spiritual Beliefs

*We are not human beings having a spiritual experience;
we are spiritual beings having a human experience.*

—Pierre Teilhard de Chardin

Spiritual Beliefs Quiz

How satisfied are you with your spiritual beliefs as a couple?

You can take this Spiritual Beliefs Quiz alone and see how you score individually using the format and scoring at the end of the chapter.

Encourage your partner to also take the Spiritual Beliefs Quiz so you can identify your strengths and issues regarding spiritual beliefs as a couple. Instructions for scoring and discussing the Quiz are described at the end of the chapter in Couple Exercise 6.3.

Response Choices

1	2	3	4	5
Strongly Disagree	Disagree	Undecided	Agree	Strongly Agree

1. My partner and I agree on how to practice our spiritual beliefs.

2. Religion has different meanings for each of us.

3. My partner and I agree on the level of religious involvement we desire in our marriage.

4. Regular attendance at a place of worship is important to me.

5. Our spiritual beliefs help us feel closer as a couple.

Breathing Life into Relationships

Spirituality and faith are powerful dimensions of the human experience. Spiritual beliefs can provide a foundation for the values and behaviors of individuals and couples. But what is meant by *spiritual* can be very different both across various religious denominations and within individuals. In a broad sense, *spirituality* refers to the relationship everyone has with God, others, and self. "To speak of your spirit, then, is to speak of the power of life that is within you," writes theologian Frederick Buechner.

People who profess a spiritual faith do, indeed, feel that their beliefs breathe life into their relationships. In contrast, those whose religious upbringing was uninspiring place little importance in faith.

Nevertheless, given the potential benefits of spiritual beliefs in a relationship, it makes sense for partners to explore and evaluate their compatibility regarding spiritual beliefs. Couples with strong spiritual beliefs and practices say their faith provides a foundation that deepens their love and helps them grow together and achieve their dreams. Even if partners hold dissimilar views, they can still have a committed, strong spiritual life that adds meaning and purpose to their existence.

Common Stumbling Blocks in Spiritual Beliefs

The most common differences for couples in terms of spiritual beliefs, according to our national survey of 21,501 married couples, are summarized in Table 6.1. In comparison to other relationship issues, spiritual beliefs have a low overall disagreement rate among married couples. In part, that may be because both spouses agree that spirituality either has a high or low priority in their lives.

The most common disagreement item regarding spirituality involves resolving differences in their spiritual beliefs. More than half of all spouses (53%) disagree on this item. Half of the spouses disagree that religious beliefs make them feel closer. Almost half (48%) of them disagree that they rely on their spiritual beliefs during difficult times, and that they are satisfied with how they express their spiritual beliefs and values. Some couples (38%) report that spiritual differences cause tension in their relationship.

Table 6.1 Top Five Stumbling Blocks regarding Spiritual Beliefs

RELIGIOUS ISSUE	PERCENTAGE OF COUPLES HAVING PROBLEM
1. We have not resolved the differences in our spiritual beliefs.	53%
2. We do not feel closer as a result of our spiritual beliefs.	50
3. We do not rely on our spiritual beliefs during difficult times.	48
4. We are dissatisfied with how we express our spiritual values and beliefs.	48
5. Spiritual differences cause tension in our relationship.	36

Differing Ways of Practicing Faith

Spouses often have different desires and values with regard to how they want to express their faith. One partner may value regular place of worship attendance, while the other may feel that spirituality is not necessarily linked to attendance at a place of worship. In our national survey, the key factor that distinguished happy and unhappy couples in terms of religion was agreement on satisfaction with how spiritual values and beliefs are expressed. Most happily married couples (89%) agree on this item, compared with only 36% of unhappily married couples.

Religion not Integrated into Couple Relationship

Often spiritual beliefs are practiced individually and not integrated into the couple relationship. Although spirituality can also be regarded as a private matter, we know that shared religious faith can strengthen a marriage. Table 6.2 summarizes our research on happily versus unhappily married couples in terms of spiritual beliefs. Happily married couples are much more likely (85%) than unhappily married couples (46%) to report that shared religious values improve their relationship. Happily married couples also more often report that they feel closer as a couple because of shared spiritual beliefs.

Lack of Discussion of Religious Beliefs

Like sex and money, religion is particularly difficult for people to talk about. Spiritual beliefs often are not discussed directly by partners. Although partners may find it difficult to share their feelings and attitudes about religious issues, communication is vital to mutual understanding. In particular, interfaith relationships require tolerance and understanding on both parts. Issues such as what faith to raise children in and how to deal with relatives, rituals, and holidays can be especially problematic if they have not been discussed. Communication is particularly important in order to enhance shared spiritual meanings and to integrate faith into a marriage.

Strengths of Happy Couples

Without faith, nothing is possible. With it, nothing is impossible.
—Mary McLeod Bethune

Research has documented the benefits of faith and congregational support in individual well-being (Walsh, 1999). There is also evidence of the positive role that religion plays in marriage (Bock & Radelet, 1988). A recent study found that couples who integrate religion into their marriage have less marital conflict, more verbal collaboration, greater marital adjustment, and more perceived benefits from marriage (Mahoney et al, 1999).

Beliefs Providing Meaning to Life

Many people say their faith is part of a personal mission upon which they base their actions. For them, religion provides a context and perspective that keeps them focused on long-term goals rather than short-term gratification. Their beliefs guide their daily actions with regard to morality, integrity, relationships, love, finances, and more.

A shared spiritual relationship can provide a significant foundation for a growing marital relationship. Even if spouses do not hold the same religious views, they can still have a committed, strong faith life that gives them the sense of serving a higher purpose. In a real sense, God's unconditional love is a model for their partnership. Their faith helps them focus on the positive aspects of each other and to encourage and respect each other. Their marriage is a sanctuary—a source of care, mutual protection, comfort, and refuge. When feelings change, their faith tides them over and sustains the relationship.

Table 6.2 Strengths of Happy versus Unhappy Couples regarding Spirituality

| | PERCENTAGE IN AGREEMENT | |
SPIRITUAL ISSUE	HAPPY COUPLES	UNHAPPY COUPLES
1. We are satisfied with how we express our spiritual values and beliefs.	89%	36%
2. We feel closer because of shared spiritual beliefs.	79	40
3. Shared spiritual beliefs improve our relationship.	85	46
4. Spiritual differences do not cause tension in our relationship.	90	54
5. We rely on our spiritual beliefs during difficult times.	79	43

Participation in Faith Communities

People who attend worship services and participate in a religious community enjoy a sense of belonging to something larger than their own family. Faith communities embrace and support couples, helping them stay focused on their goals and ideals. Regular worship becomes a life source that renews and restores them, gives them a sense of community, and provides a context for action.

As Bruce and Stan write in *God Is in the Small Stuff for Your Family*, "Faith communities act as families that provide the exuberance of the young and wisdom of the mature. Within this context of diversity, you can appreciate qualities, experiences and opinions of people with perspectives different than your own."

A Refuge in Times of Crisis

No one is immune to sadness, loss, or grief. Tough times may drain us physically or emotionally, but faith and prayer can be powerful weapons in times of emotional crisis.

Depending on the response, tragedy can splinter a family or bring it together. In times of grief, people often form deep and lasting bonds within their family and religious community. Faith and prayer in your couple relationship can be great resources during difficult times, as well as building blocks to intimacy.

An Expanding Definition of Spirituality

*The best and most beautiful things in the world cannot be seen
or even touched. They must be felt with the heart.*

—Helen Keller (1880–1968)

Many people who have developed a close relationship with God acknowledge God's presence and activity in their lives. They pay close attention to those small, uplifting experiences that are part of daily life. They expand the definition of spirituality to include ordinary but life-affirming moments. Life viewed from this perspective is rich and fulfilling. And embracing the spiritual meaning and experience with your partner can have a powerful positive influence on your relationship.

Couple Exercise 6.1
Exploring your Past

How much do you know about your partner's religious history? How much do you know about your own religious history? Family heritage lends a sense of stability and tranquility to relationships.

Set aside some time to discuss the following questions. If you do not have the answers, ask other family members or visit the historical society.

1. What is your family's ethnicity?

2. What is the origin of your family name? (In Biblical times, names often were connected to race or profession.)

3. What is your family's religion?

4. What holidays (holy days) and rituals do you and your partner currently celebrate?

5. Where did those celebrations originate?

6. What do holiday symbols mean, like the Menorah and Christmas tree?

7. Is there significance to the food you prepare?

8. What is the meaning of the gifts you exchange?

Through rituals, we create a treasure chest of memories, communicate information about values, and build a family legacy for our children and grandchildren. With that in mind, create a new family or couple ritual. Then integrate it into your weekly, monthly, or yearly routines.

Couple Exercise 6.2
Celebrating the Small Stuff

Set aside a quiet time. Light a few candles or start a fire in the fireplace, and sit down with your partner. Try one or both of the following exercises.

1. *Write down three uplifting moments when you felt energized during the last month.* Picture those moments when you felt most alive—when the commonplace became not so commonplace, such as the slant of late winter rays of sunlight, good work well done, a game of touch football in the fall leaves, or rocking your child to sleep.

Now share your experiences with each other.

2. *Write down the names of the three people with whom you are most joyful. Then write down the names of the three people whom you trust the most.*

Share the names on both lists with your partner. Talk about why you trust the people you named. Discuss specific reasons you enjoy the people you named.

Couple Exercise 6.3
Discussing Your Strengths and Growth Areas
in Spiritual Beliefs

TAKING SPIRITUAL BELIEFS QUIZ:
Each partner should take this Spiritual Beliefs Quiz and record your responses below.

IDENTIFY YOUR COUPLE STRENGTHS:
Strengths are the items where you both agree with each other. On items 1, 3, 4 and 5, circle those items if you both agreed (response 4 or 5). On item 2, circle it if you both disagreed (response 1 or 2). *Circle the Strength items you identified.*

COUPLE DISCUSSION:
1. Discuss your Strengths and be proud of them.
2. Discuss the other items and decide how you can turn them into strengths.

Response Choices

1	2	3	4	5
Strongly Disagree	Disagree	Undecided	Agree	Strongly Agree

	PARTNER 1	PARTNER 2
1. My partner and I agree on how to practice our spiritual beliefs.	_____	_____
2. Religion has different meanings for each of us.	_____	_____
3. My partner and I agree on the level of religious involvement we desire in our marriage.	_____	_____
4. Regular attendance at a place of worship is important to me.	_____	_____
5. Our spiritual beliefs help us feel closer as a couple.	_____	_____

Scoring of the Quiz

1. Individually take the quiz.

2. Score the quiz as follows:
    a. Total your points for items 1, 3, 4, and 5. _____
    b. Add 6 to the total of a. __+ 6__
    c. Total points for item 2. _____
    d. Subtract c from b. _____

    PARTNER 1:_____   PARTNER 2: _____

3. Interpreting your score: Range = 5–25

    21–25 = You have very compatible spiritual beliefs.
    15–20 = You have compatible spiritual beliefs.
    11–14 = You have somewhat compatible spiritual beliefs.
     5–10 = You have somewhat incompatible spiritual beliefs.

4. After you have both taken and scored the Quiz, compare how you perceive
    your relationship regarding spiritual beliefs.

Suggestions for Improving
Your Spiritual Beliefs

1. Take time to learn about your partner's view of spirituality.

2. Integrate aspects of your spiritual lives into your couple relationship.

3. Establish some rituals that will honor your spiritual beliefs.

**Turn your stumbling blocks
into stepping stones!**

Chapter Seven

Sexual Relationship

The war between the sexes is the only one in which both sides regularly sleep with the enemy.

—Quentin Crisp

Sexual Relationship Quiz

How satisfied are you with your sexual relationship as a couple?

You can take this Sexual Relationship Quiz alone and see how you score individually using the format and scoring at the end of the chapter.

Encourage your partner to also take the Sexual Relationship Quiz so you can identify your strengths and issues regarding sexual relationship as a couple. Instructions for scoring and discussing the Quiz are described at the end of the chapter in Couple Exercise 7.2.

Response Choices

1	2	3	4	5
Strongly Disagree	Disagree	Undecided	Agree	Strongly Agree

1. I am satisfied with the amount of affection my partner gives me.

2. We have similar sexual interests and expectations.

3. My partner uses or refuses sex in an unfair way.

4. We have difficulty keeping our sexual relationship interesting and enjoyable.

5. It is easy for us to talk about our sexual relationship.

What Sex Reveals and Conceals

The sexual relationship acts as the emotional barometer for the relationship in that it can reflect a couple's satisfaction with other aspects of the relationship. A good sexual relationship is often the outcome of a good emotional relationship between the partners. Paradoxically, sex can also suppress the expression of deeper concerns and issues. This is because sex is one of the most difficult topics for individuals to discuss and to share personal feelings about. Some couples try to use sex to "smooth over" disputes. This may seem to be the easier alternative to actually talking about and working through issues, but it is never more than a temporary solution to an underlying problem.

Because sexuality affects other aspects of a relationship, the sexual relationship tends to be a good gauge of the overall health and well being of your relationship.

Couples who have a good emotional connection have the best physical relationship. For them, sexuality flows from emotional intimacy based on open and honest communication. A marriage that is characterized by a lack of trust, that is stressed with financial concerns, or that is plagued with destructive conflict is probably not sexually satisfying for either partner.

In their classic study of 5,945 couples, Blumstein and Schwartz (1983) discovered that couples who fought about such things as parenting, household responsibilities, or finances tended to have less satisfying sexual relationships.

Common Stumbling Blocks to a Satisfying Sexual Relationship

Sexuality is an area in which differences in husband and wife preferences are more common and problematic. Our national survey of 21,501 married couples revealed data on sexual issues for couples; Table 7.1 summarizes the findings. The most problematic sexual issue for couples is dissatisfaction with the amount of affection received. A majority of couples also disagree that their sexual relationship is satisfying and fulfilling and disagree in finding ways to keep the sexual relationship interesting. More than half of couples have difficulties discussing sexual issues openly. And half of the couples report reluctance to be affectionate with a partner because the partner often interprets affection as a sexual advance.

Table 7.1 Top Five Stumbling Blocks regarding Sexuality

SEXUAL ISSUE	PERCENTAGE OF COUPLES HAVING PROBLEM
1. I am dissatisfied with the amount of affection from my partner.	70%
2. We work to keep our sexual relationship interesting and enjoyable.	62
3. Our sexual relationship is not satisfying or fulfilling.	57
4. I am dissatisfied with the level of openness in discussing sexual topics.	54
5. I am reluctant to be affectionate because my partner may interpret it as a sexual advance.	50

Different Levels of Sexual Interest

The movie *Annie Hall* depicts two lovers with different perceptions of their sexual relationship. When a therapist asks them (separately) how often they have sex, the character played by Woody Allen answers, *"Hardly ever, maybe three times a week."* The character played by Diane Keaton replies, *"Constantly, three times a week."*

Among married couples, the most common sexual concern stems from differing interests in sex. Studies have shown that, for a majority of men, sex can be easily separated from the relationship. For instance, if he is angry at her for spending more time at the office than she spends at home, he still may be interested in sex. But women tend to view sex from a relational perspective. For instance, if she is angry at him for forgetting to run some errands he had promised to take care of, she may not feel affectionate toward him. Feelings of emotional intimacy in the relationship usually precede sexual expression for women, whereas males often view sex as a way to increase intimacy.

Lack of Affection from the Partner

Love is an irresistible desire to be irresistibly desired.

—Robert Frost (1874–1963)

Spouses often are not satisfied with the affection they receive from their partner. We know that this is a very important component to a happy marriage, because it was also the highest discriminator between happily and unhappily married couples (in 72% of happily married couples, partners report being satisfied with the affection they get from each other, versus only 28% of unhappy couples).

When newspaper columnist Ann Landers polled her readers on their thoughts and feelings about sex, 72% of the 90,000 women said they'd be content to be held lovingly rather than actually have sex. Although this was not a scientifically conducted study, it certainly highlights the importance of affection.

Difficulty Talking About Sexual Relationship

The process of talking about sex and feelings about sex can be very difficult, even for married couples. One reason for this is that we rarely have had models for talking about sex. Sex was most likely something you did not frequently discuss with your parents, or even your friends, while growing up. Because of this, sexual issues acquire a taboo-like quality.

In fact, over half of all married couples find it difficult to discuss sexual issues. There is a significant discrepancy in the ability to discuss sexuality between happily and unhappily married couples. In only 34% of unhappily married couples do partners report satisfaction in talking about sexual issues, compared with 83% of happily married couples. Therefore, the ability to communicate about sex is important in developing and maintaining both sexual and relationship satisfaction.

Sexual Strengths of Happy Couples

A major strength for happily married couples is the quality of the sexual relationship. In our national survey of married couples, we discovered distinct differences between happy and unhappy couples in terms of their sexual relationship (Table 7.2). Individuals in happy marriages are much more satisfied with the amount of affection they receive from their partner than unhappily married couples are. They also agree that their sexual relationship is satisfying and fulfilling, and they are much more likely to agree that their partner does not use or refuse sex in an unfair way. Further, they are far less likely to feel concerned that their partner is not interested in them sexually. Finally, they agree much more often that they are not worried that their partner may have thought about having a sexual relationship outside of their marriage.

Table 7.2 Strengths of Happy Versus Unhappy Couples regarding Sexuality

| | PERCENTAGE IN AGREEMENT | |
| | HAPPY | UNHAPPY |
SEXUALITY ISSUE	COUPLES	COUPLES
1. I am completely satisfied with the affection from my partner.	72%	28%
2. Our sexual relationship is satisfying and fulfilling.	85	29
3. My partner does not use or refuse sex in an unfair way.	90	39
4. I have no concerns that my partner may not be interested in me sexually.	88	37
5. I am not worried that my partner has thought about having an affair.	92	43

Improved Communication

Different people have different needs for sexual intimacy, and those needs affect how they perceive their sexual behavior. This is one of the reasons couples must communicate clearly about sex if they are to maintain a satisfying relationship. In terms of different levels of sexual interest, communicating will facilitate an understanding of your partner's perspective, which will strengthen the bonds and increase the intimacy between you.

Suggestions for Improving Your Sexual Health

1. Always remember that good sex begins while your clothes are still on.

2. Take time to think about yourself as a sexual being.

3. Take responsibility for your own sexual pleasure.

4. Talk with your partner about sex.

5. Make time to be together regularly.

6. Don't let sex become routine.

7. Use fantasy—you'll find it's one of the best aphrodisiacs.

8. Understand that working at sex doesn't work.

9. Don't carry anger into your bedroom.

10. Realize that good sex isn't just a matter of pushing the right buttons.

11. Nurture the romance in your life.

12. Don't make sex too serious.

13. Don't always wait to be "in the mood" before agreeing to have sex.

14. Realize that you and your partner don't have to see eye to eye sexually.

15. Don't be afraid to ask for help.

16. Try to keep your sexual expectations realistic.

Source: Masters, Johnson, and Kolodny, 1988, (pp. 452-461).

Remember that the quality of the communication affects the quality of the relationship, and the quality of the relationship affects the quality of the sex. Refer to Chapter 2 for ways to improve communication skills, such as practicing active listening, being assertive, and using "I" statements. An easy way to build intimacy through communication is self-disclosure. Share with your partner your feelings and interests about sexual issues.

Don't forget to use touch and eye contact as a way to communicate warmth and affection. Holding hands with your partner or giving him or her a loving glance are very important ways to convey emotions nonverbally.

Tokens of Affection

If you think back to the early stages of your relationship with your partner, you may remember that giving and sharing seemed to be easy. You probably shared more positive feelings and experiences than negative ones, and you probably found many ways to express love and affection. These "tokens of affection" are just as important now as they were then. This can be as simple as calling in the middle of the day to let your partner know you are thinking of him or her.

After all, if you think about people in your life who you enjoy being around, they most likely make you feel valued and accepted. The following example illustrates how we tend to like people who make us feel special:

A young woman was explaining to a friend why she had decided to marry one man rather than another. "When I was with John," she said, "I felt he was the cleverest person in the world."

"Then why didn't you choose him?" the puzzled friend asked.

"Because when I'm with Bill I feel **I'm** *the cleverest person in the world."*

—Bits & Pieces (1997)

You may have to consciously remind yourself to give these tokens of affection—compliments, little gifts, cards, and so on. You will inevitably discover the reciprocal nature of giving, and eventually it will come from genuine desire.

Positive Action

*More people behave themselves into new ways of thinking
than think themselves into new ways of behaving.*

If you find that your marriage has lost the "spark" it used to have, you will need to make a conscious, focused effort to increase the emotional and physical temperature of the relationship. When it comes to taking action in terms of implementing these ideas into your lives, just do it! Give your spouse a genuine compliment, hold his hand, do her a favor. Every day, go out of your way to do something kind and affectionate.

You may be surprised to find that, by changing your actions or your motions, your emotions will change as well. We often make the mistake of believing that we have to have the feeling before we can take the action. This is not necessary.

In fact, by changing your actions, you will also change your emotions. And once you get back into the habit of making your spouse feel valued and special, it will feel natural. Like anything worthwhile, this takes some effort, but the results are well worth the effort.

Couple Exercise 7.1
Planning a Romantic Adventure

Make a plan to spend some quality time together. This "adventure" can be whatever pleases both of you and fits into your lives and interests. Schedule and organize this in advance, following these guidelines:

1. Be realistic.
2. Plan something that you will be able to do in the next few months.
3. Plan something that is not too expensive.
4. Answer these questions:
   a. When?

   _____

   b. Where?

   _____

   c. What can you each contribute to make it happen?

   _____
   _____
   _____
   _____
   _____

Couple Exercise 7.2
Discussing Your Strengths and
Growth Areas in Sexual Relationship

TAKING SEXUAL RELATIONSHIP QUIZ:

Each partner should take this Sexual Relationship Quiz and record your responses below.

IDENTIFY YOUR COUPLE STRENGTHS:

Strengths are the items where you both agree with each other. On items 1, 2 and 5, circle those items if you both agreed (response 4 or 5). On items 3 and 4, circle the items if you both disagreed (response 1 or 2). *Circle the Strength items you identified.*

COUPLE DISCUSSION:

1. Discuss your Strengths and be proud of them.
2. Discuss the other items and decide how you can turn them into strengths.

Response Choices				
1	2	3	4	5
Strongly Disagree	Disagree	Undecided	Agree	Strongly Agree

	PARTNER 1	PARTNER 2
1. I am satisfied with the amount of affection my partner gives me.	_____	_____
2. We have similar sexual interests and expectations.	_____	_____
3. My partner uses or refuses sex in an unfair way.	_____	_____
4. We have difficulty keeping our sexual relationship interesting and enjoyable.	_____	_____
5. It is easy for us to talk about our sexual relationship.	_____	_____

━━━━━━━━━ Scoring of the Quiz ━━━━━━━━━

1. Individually take the quiz.

2. Score the quiz as follows:
   a. Total your points for items 1, 2, and 5.   _____
   b. Add 12 to total of a.   __+12__
   c. Total points for items 3 and 4.   _____
   d. Subtract c from b.   _____

   PARTNER 1:_____   PARTNER 2: _____

3. Interpreting your score: Range = 5–25

   21–25 = You are very satisfied with your sexual relationship.
   15–20 = You are satisfied with your sexual relationship.
   11–14 = You are generally satisfied with your sexual relationship.
    5–10 = You are dissatisfied with your sexual relationship.

4. After you have both taken and scored the Quiz, compare how you perceive
   your relationship regarding sexual issues.

Suggestions for Improving Your Sexual Relationship

1. Remember the importance of being affectionate aside from being sexual.

2. Discuss your different levels of sexual interest.

3. Let your partner know he or she is valued and appreciated.

4. Remember that improving the emotional connection with your partner will consequently improve your physical connection.

**Turn your stumbling blocks
into stepping stones!**

Chapter Eight

Mapping Your Couple Relationship

In your couple relationship, you either repeat what you learned in your family or you tend to do the opposite.

—David H. Olson

Couple Relationship Quiz

How satisfied are you with your closeness and flexibility as a couple?

You can take this Couple Relationship Quiz alone and see how you score individually using the format and scoring at the end of chapter.

Encourage your partner to also take the Couple Relationship Quiz so you can identify your strengths and issues regarding closeness and flexibility as a couple. Instructions for scoring and discussing the Quiz are described at the end of chapter in Couple Exercise 8.2.

Couple Closeness

1. How often do you spend free time together?

1	2	3	4	5
Never	Seldom	Sometimes	Often	Very Often

2. How committed are you to your partner?

1	2	3	4	5
Slightly	Somewhat	Generally	Very	Extremely

3. How close do you feel to your partner?

1	2	3	4	5
Not very close	Somewhat close	Generally close	Very close	Extremely close

4. How do you and your partner balance separateness and togetherness?

1	2	3	4	5
Mainly separateness	More separateness than togetherness`	Equal togetherness and separateness	More togetherness than separateness	Mainly togetherness

5. How independent of or dependent on each other are you and your partner?

1	2	3	4	5
Very independent	More independent than dependent	Equally dependent and independent	More dependent than independent	Very dependent

Add your responses to these questions to get a total closeness score.

Couple Flexibility

1. What kind of leadership is there in your couple relationship?

1	2	3	4	5
One person usually leads	Leadership is sometimes shared	Leadership is generally shared	Leadership is usually shared	Leadership is unclear

2. How often do you and your partner do the same things (roles) around the house?

1	2	3	4	5
Almost always	Usually	Often	Sometimes	Seldom

3. What are the rules (written or unwritten) like in your family?

1	2	3	4	5
Rules very clear and very stable	Rules clear and generally stable	Rules clear and structured	Rules clear and flexible	Rules unclear and changing

4. How are decisions handled?

1	2	3	4	5
One person usually decides	Decisions are sometimes shared	Decisions are often shared	Decisions are usually shared	Decisions are rarely made

5. How much change occurs in your couple relationship?

1	2	3	4	5
Very little change	Little change	Some change	Considerable change	A great deal of change

Add your responses to these questions to get a total flexibility score.

Figure 8.1 Couple and Family Map

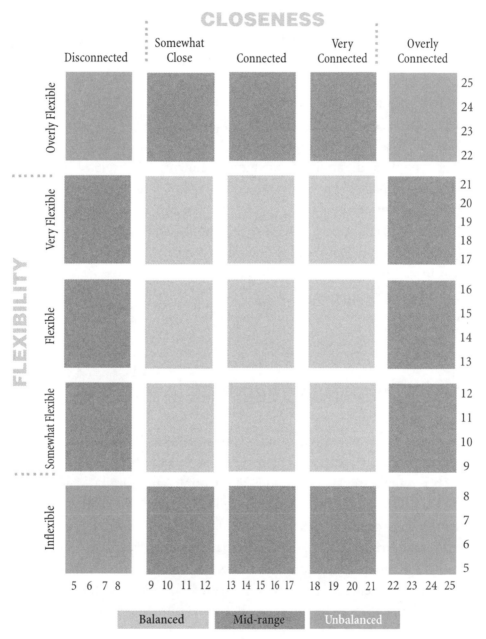

The Couple and Family Map

Whether you were raised in a small or large family or by one or two parents and whether you lived with biological, step-, half- or no siblings, your family was unique in its makeup and functioning. When you consider all the facets of families and the complex, interconnected relationships within them, you will realize that no two are truly alike. The fact that families are so diverse can add to the challenge of merging individuals from two families in a couple relationship.

The Couple and Family Map, which is shown in Figure 8.1, helps you describe and visually depict both your couple relationship and family of origin. It enables you to see the linkage between your couple relationship and your family of origin, which otherwise may not be so obvious.

The Couple and Family Map identifies twenty-five different styles of relationships. Based on your results on the Couple Quiz (pages 139-140,) you can plot your scores on the Map using the "Assessing your Couple and Family Type" section of this chapter (pages 151-153.)

Couple and Family Closeness

Closeness refers to how emotionally connected you feel to another person. It involves how you balance separateness and togetherness— your private space and your intimate connection. The Couple and Family Map breaks closeness into five levels, from disconnected at the lowest level, to connected in the middle, to overly connected on the high end (See Figure 8.2).

Finding the right balance between separateness and togetherness is the key to healthy couple and family closeness. Although being disconnected (too much separateness) or overly connected (too much togetherness) can be appropriate at times, relationships that always operate at these extremes tend to be unhealthy.

Figure 8.2 Five Levels of Closeness
Balancing Separateness vs. Togetherness

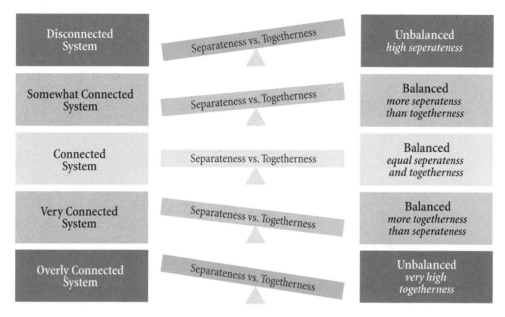

It is normal for couple and family relationships to shift back and forth between togetherness and separateness depending on what is happening in the relationship. But couples and families that get locked into an unbalanced level of closeness (too much or too little) tend to have more problems.

Balancing Separateness and Togetherness

Couples and families that maintain a happy, healthy relationship strike a good balance between spending time together and separately. In these families, each member develops both some dependence on the family and some independence of his or her own. This kind of balance is a comfortable one in which members can move back and forth between separateness and togetherness with ease. Of course, sometimes things will get out of balance, and that's OK—as long as you do not get stuck there.

Kahlil Gibran describes a balance between separateness and togetherness in his poem "On Marriage":

> *Love one another, but make not a bond of love:*
> *Let it rather be a moving sea between the shores of your souls.*
> *Sing and dance together and be joyous, but let each one of you be alone,*
> *Even as the strings of a lute are alone though they quiver with the same*
> *music.*
> *Give your hearts, but not into each other's keeping.*
> *For only the hand of Life can contain your hearts.*
> *And stand together yet not too near together:*
> *For the pillars of the temple stand apart,*
> *And the oak tree and the cypress grow not in each other's shadow.*
> *But let there be spaces in your togetherness,*
> *And let the winds of the heavens dance between you.*
>
> —(1923/1976, pp. 16–17)

The relationship Gibran describes is an ideal balance between separateness and togetherness. Finding this kind of balance takes time, hard work, and commitment. In cohesive relationships, individuals place emphasis on the "self" as well as the "we." They strive for an appropriate amount of sharing, loyalty, intimacy, and independence. They learn how to balance their development as individuals with the growth of the relationship.

Table 8.1 Strengths of Happy Versus Unhappy Couples regarding Couple Closeness

| | PERCENTAGE IN AGREEMENT | |
| | HAPPY | UNHAPPY |
RELATIONSHIP ISSUE	COUPLES	COUPLES
1. We feel very close to each other.	98%	27%
2. Our togetherness is a top priority for us.	88	28
3. We ask each other for help.	96	40
4. We find it easy to think of things to do together.	86	28
5. We really enjoy spending our free time together.	97	43

When happy couples were compared with unhappy couples in our national survey, there were distinct differences between the two samples in couple closeness; Table 8.1 summarizes the key findings. For instance, members of almost all of the happy couples agree that they feel very close to their partner, whereas only 27% of unhappy couples feel that way. Partners in happy couples are also more than three times as likely as unhappy couples to agree that they find it easy to think of things to do together.

Avoiding Extreme Separateness or Closeness

Figure 8.2 depicts five levels of couple and family closeness. Having a very low or a very high level of closeness can eventually lead to problems. When a relationship is "disconnected"—not close—the individuals tend to focus more on themselves than on each other. They tend to have too much separateness and to be highly independent. They may feel that they cannot count on their relationship to give them support when they need it. This extreme separateness depicted in Figure 8.2 is labeled "disconnected." Fritz Perls expressed the idea of extreme separateness in the "Gestalt Prayer":

> *I do my thing, and you do your thing.*
> *I am not in this world to live up to your expectations.*
> *And you are not in this world to live up to mine.*
> *You are you and I am I.*
>
> —(1969, p. 4)

Successful couples and families tend to be those that have achieved an appropriate balance between the "I" and "we." Individuals maintain both their own individuality and their closeness. "Overly connected" relationships—with an extreme amount of closeness are not ideal either. In these relationships, members can have too much togetherness, demand loyalty, be too dependent on one another, and have little private time or space. The needs of the relationship often come before the needs of the individuals, and it may be difficult for some family members to accept people outside of the family in interpersonal relationships with other family members. Judy Altura has expressed extreme closeness in her "Togetherness Poem":

> *We do everything together.*
> *I am here to meet all your needs and expectations.*
> *And you are here to meet mine.*
> *We had to meet, and it was beautiful.*
> *I can't imagine it turning out any other way.*
>
> —(1974, p. 20)

Couple and Family Flexibility

Flexibility refers to how open to change couples and families are in their relationships. It describes the amount of change that occurs, for example, in leadership, role relationships, and relationship rules. As with closeness, there are five levels of flexibility: from inflexible on the low end, to flexible in the

Figure 8.3 Five Levels of Flexibility: Balancing Stability and Change

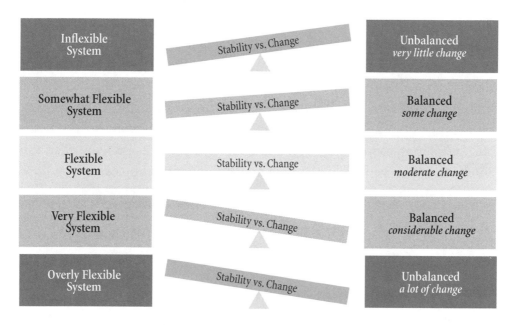

middle, to overly flexible on the high end. Again, the two extremes can work within relationships in the short run, but over time they are unhealthy. The flexibility component on the Couple and Family Map assesses how the couple or family system balances stability and change (See Figure 8.3).

Balancing Stability and Change

Balancing the flexibility in your couple and family relationships is an important aspect, too. Since change is inevitable, individual's relationships must be open to it. But people also want and need stability. Without stability, they cannot develop intimacy in their relationships. Relationships that have an "appropriate" level of flexibility are somewhat structured, and members sometimes share leadership. Roles are well defined and stable, but they can change depending on current needs. Flexibility becomes vital in times of crisis, as members adapt to changing conditions and roles while coping with stress. Relationships that function well at these times are still considered balanced because they operate in one of the extremes for only a short period of time before returning to a more equal state.

When happy and unhappy couples' relationship flexibility were compared, some clear differences emerged, although they were not as pronounced as differences in levels of closeness; Table 8.2 summarizes the findings. For instance, happy couples agree more often than unhappy couples to being creative in handling differences and adjusting to necessary change. Happy couples also agree to making more decisions together and compromising when problems arise than do unhappy couples.

Table 8.2 Strengths of Happy Versus Unhappy Couples regarding Flexibility

| | PERCENTAGE IN AGREEMENT | |
RELATIONSHIP ISSUE	HAPPY COUPLES	UNHAPPY COUPLES
1. We are creative in how we handle our differences.	78%	55%
2. We make most decisions jointly.	54	33
3. Both of us are able to adjust to change when it's necessary.	64	42
4. We are flexible in our lifestyle.	59	38
5. We compromise when problems arise.	68	47

Avoiding Extreme Stability or Change

Figure 8.3 depicts five levels of family stability. Couples and families very low on flexibility can be described as "inflexible." In an inflexible relationship, rules rarely change, even to accommodate special situations and normal life changes. In these relationships, people rarely negotiate, roles are very stable, and discipline is strict. They often are characterized by authoritarian leadership.

At the other extreme are "overly flexible" relationships. In overly flexible relationships, there is often so much change that these families function almost completely without structure, roles, or rules. Excessive change is disruptive and leads to feelings of insecurity within the family. When rules and roles frequently change, things do not get done, and the lack of order limits the productivity within the family. Overly flexible relationships are off balance and feel chaotic because of so much change.

Exploring Your Family of Origin

There are no individuals in the world.
Only fragments of families.

—Carl Whitaker

Your family of origin—the family you grew up in—still has a powerful influence in your current life. Your family is, therefore, very much alive in your relationships. What you saw and experienced growing up shapes many of your expectations. Particularly when responsibilities and stress increase, you will tend to revert to the scripts you learned and followed in your upbringing.

Gaining a deeper understanding of your family of origin will help you to understand yourself and your partner better. You may be surprised to find that certain attitudes or beliefs originated from your early family life. And these ideas and beliefs directly affect your actions.

Take, for example, Lori and Tim, a married couple. In Lori's family, everyone was expected to be present at dinnertime. Lori's family used this time for family members to socialize and reconnect with one another. Lori has many fond memories of shared dinners—laughing, talking, and discussing family issues during this time.

In contrast, Tim's family did not place much importance on shared meal-times. Since his was a large family, and individuals had different schedules, even if dinner was prepared, family members often came and went as they pleased. It was even common for family members to grab a plate of food and watch the evening news or even retreat to their bedrooms.

What do you suppose happened with Lori and Tim in regard to dinner meals together? Not surprisingly, their different experiences and values about dinnertime caused some initial problems. Lori expected that she and Tim would be together during dinner, whereas for Tim this was not a priority. He wondered why Lori seemed so withdrawn if he stayed late at the office or decided to go out with his teammates after their company softball games. And Lori also felt upset if Tim watched television while he ate, since she hoped they would have a conversation.

Although this is a fairly nonthreatening example of how our families of origin can affect us, there are unlimited potential differences that could cause even more serious problems for couples. And many times it is not the big things that cause a decline in the quality of relationships but the many little things, which eventually affect couples in big ways.

Assessing your Couple and Family Type

The following Couple Exercise 8.1 (page 152) focuses on your couple relationship and Couple Exercise 8.2 (page 154) focuses on your family of origin. Each exercise will help you improve your relationship.

In general, if you fall into one of the center six quadrants, your relationship is balanced in terms of connectedness and flexibility. You will be able to see the specific level of closeness and flexibility in the relationship you described. Balanced relationships usually are happier and healthier.

If you fall into one of the twelve midrange (darker shaded) areas, your relationships may sometimes be unbalanced and other times be in balance. This inconsistency can lead to problems in the long term.

If you fall into one of the four corners, your relationship probably is unbalanced in terms of both closeness and flexibility. These extreme patterns tend to be more problematic, one or both partners tend to be more unhappy. A more balanced approach to cohesion and flexibility is best for relationships as they grow and change over time.

Couple Exercise 8.1
Exercise on Couple Map

1. Complete the Couple Relationship Quiz at the beginning of the chapter for how your relationship is *Now*. You can take the same Quiz again to describe how you would *Ideally* like your couple relationship to be.

2. Score the quiz for both the "now" and the "ideal." Then plot both scores onto the Couple and Family Map (See Figure 8.4).

		CLOSENESS	FLEXIBILITY
Partner 1	Now	_____	_____
	Ideal	_____	_____
Partner 2	Now	_____	_____
	Ideal	_____	_____

3. Compare how you each described your relationship *Now* on the Couple and Family Map. Discuss similarities and differences on couple closeness and couple flexibility.

4. Compare how you each described how you would *Ideally* like your relationship to be. Discuss similarities and differences.

5. Discuss how you can work together to make your relationship more like the Ideals.

Figure 8.4 Couple and Family Map

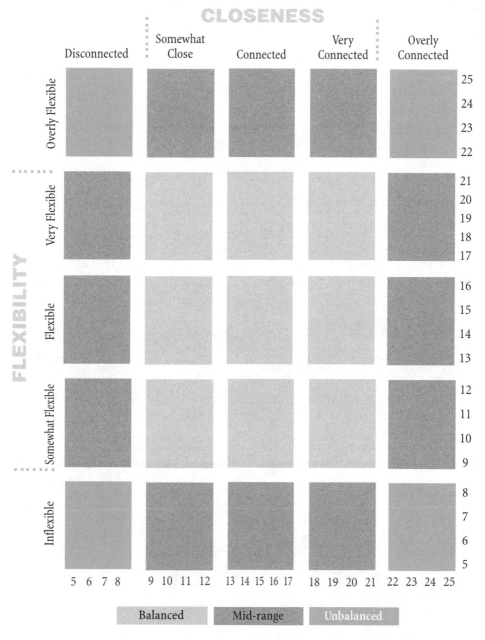

Couple Exercise 8.2
Comparing Your Family of Origin

1. Individually, locate and plot where you think your family of origin would be located on the Couple and Family Map.

2. Compare your family of origin with the family of origin of your partner in terms of closeness and flexibility.

   a. Closeness

   1) How similar or different were your families in terms of closeness?

   2) How do the similarities or differences impact your current relationship?

   3) What from your family of origin would you like to repeat and what would you not like to repeat in your current couple relationship?

   b. Flexibility

   1) How similar or different were your families in terms of flexibility?

   2) How do the similarities or differences impact your current relationship?

   3) What from your family or origin would you like to repeat and what would you not like to repeat in your current couple relationship?

Suggestions for Improving Your Couple Dynamics

1. If you are not happy with the closeness in your relationship, talk about how you can achieve a more satisfying balance of separateness and togetherness.

2. If you are not happy with the flexibility of your relationship, discuss how you can achieve a more satisfying balance of stability and change.

3. Remember that communication is the facilitating factor for negotiating and making changes in your relationship.

4. Be aware that you will often repeat styles you learned from your family of origin, especially under stress.

**Turn your stumbling blocks
into stepping stones!**

Chapter Nine

Children and Parenting

Before I got married, I had six theories
about bringing up children;
now I have six children, and no theories.

—John Wilmot (1642–1680)

Parenting Quiz

How satisfied are you with your parenting as a couple?

You can take this Parenting Quiz alone and see how you score individually using the format and scoring at the end of chapter.

Encourage your partner to also take the Parenting Quiz so you can identify your parenting strengths and issues regarding parenting as a couple. Instructions for scoring and discussing the Quiz are described at the end of chapter in Couple Exercise 9.2.

Response Choices

1	2	3	4	5
Strongly Disagree	Disagree	Undecided	Agree	Strongly Agree

1. The father is actively involved in childrearing and parenting.

2. We're satisfied with how we discipline our child(ren).

3. Parenting is stressful on our marriage.

4. We give more attention to our children than our marriage.

5. We are satisfied with how we share parenting.

Joys and Demands of Parenting

The first half of our lives is spoiled by our parents,
and the last half by our children.

—Jennifer James (1984)

Counselor Jennifer James' humorous, if cynical, remark that "the first half of our lives is spoiled by our parents, and the last half by our children" (James, 1984) is one that many parents can relate to. At the same time, parents often attribute their greatest joy in life to raising children.

Paradoxically, parenting can be the most frustrating and the most satisfying experience in our lives. Parents are primarily responsible for children's development of self-esteem, sense of responsibility, values, and physical and emotional health, as well as for their social and economic needs. In spite of the monumental responsibilities associated with parenthood, people receive little, if any, training in parenting. Fortunately, awareness of the long-term significance of parenting and family relationships has led to the recent development of school curriculums focusing on these issues.

It would seem as if parenting should become easier as children grow older and become more self-reliant. But what usually happens is that circumstances change and parenting becomes more difficult as children exert their independence. Adolescence represents the most challenging stage for most parents, because teenagers are seeking greater autonomy and freedom from parental control.

Stumbling Blocks to Effective Parenting

If it was going to be easy raising kids,
it never would have started with something called labor.

—Bits and Pieces (November 6, 1997)

The major parenting issues for our national sample of 21,501 married couples with children are identified in Table 9.1. The most problematic parenting issue that couples report is feeling less satisfied in their marriage since having children. Over two-thirds of married couples report that the father does not spend enough time with the children. Almost as many couples do not agree on how to discipline their children and are dissatisfied with how child-care responsibilities are shared. Finally, many couples are dissatisfied with the balance of attention given to their marriage versus the attention given to the children.

Table 9.1 Top Five Stumbling Blocks regarding Parenting

PARENTING ISSUE	PERCENTAGE OF COUPLES HAVING PROBLEM
1. Having child(ren) has reduced our marital satisfaction.	84%
2. The father is not involved enough with our child(ren).	68
3. I am dissatisfied with how childrearing is shared.	66
4. We disagree on discipline.	66
5. My partner focuses more on the children than on the marriage.	64

Strain on the Couple Relationship

Although parenting can be fulfilling and highly rewarding, children can represent a source of tension and restrict opportunities for couples. Parenting is one of the most challenging and stressful areas for couples. Over four-fifths of the married couples in our national survey report feeling less satisfied in their marriage since having children. Even happily married couples are not immune from the stresses and strains associated with childrearing. Less than two-fifths of happily married couples report that children do not create major problems in their marriage.

The fact that children take priority over the marital relationship helps account for this decrease in marital satisfaction. Partners often do not take time to talk with each other about this. Two other reasons for a decrease in marital satisfaction are a lack of husband involvement in childrearing and disagreements on how to discipline children.

Lack of Husband Involvement

The sacrifices related to parenting are felt mostly by mothers. Women adapt their careers, sacrifice their free time, and otherwise adjust their lives to accommodate children considerably more than husbands. In our national survey, a majority of both husbands and wives report that the father does not spend enough time with the children.

Part of the problem is that men feel that their responsibilities primarily lie outside of the home. They often did not have a good role model in their own youth with a father actively involved in his children's daily lives. Some men falsely assume that childrearing is simply woman's work.

Disagreements over Discipline and Parenting Styles

A story is told about how the poet Samuel Taylor Coleridge was visited by an admirer one day. During the conversation, the subject got around to children.

"I believe," said the visitor, "that children should be given a free rein to think and act and thus learn at an early age to make their own decisions.

This is the only way they can grow into their full potential."

"Come see my flower garden," said Coleridge, leading the man outside. The visitor took one look and exclaimed, "Why, that's nothing but a yard full of weeds!"

"It used to be filled with roses," said Coleridge, "but this year I thought I'd let the garden grow as it willed without tending to it. This is the result."

Like a gardener and his or her flowers, children do not naturally do what their parents want them to do. One way to teach acceptable behavior is through fair and firm discipline. Setting limits also helps a child feel safe and secure. Unfortunately, parents often have different goals related to what behaviors they would like to reward and what behaviors they would like to discourage. And discipline that is not consistent, either with one parent or between two parents, is not effective (Brooks, 1998).

Agreeing on how to discipline children is a common problem in most marriages. All of us were parented differently, and we tend to repeat with our own children what we saw our parents do. Partners often make the mistake of not discussing their different styles, in which case they may naturally fall into the parenting style they experienced growing up.

Children Taking Priority over the Marriage

When children become the main focus of family life, the marriage can suffer. A majority (64%) of married couples report that partners give more attention to the children than to the marriage. One reason this is so common is that children are demanding—their needs are so evident. Although spouses also have needs, they just are not as apparent as the needs of their children. Also, parents may feel as if they are acting selfishly if they ask for things for themselves. Ultimately, by the time one or both parents are done taking care of the children, they have little time left for each other or for the marriage.

Parenting Strengths of Happy Couples

Our national survey of 21,501 couples identified some common views of parenting of happily and unhappily married couples; Table 9.2 summarizes the findings. Let's examine some of the findings and their consequences in detail.

Making the Couple Relationship a Priority

Although children take a lot of energy and attention, it is essential for the survival of the marriage that spouses not forget about each other and their relationship. Parenthood has an amazing way of bringing out the selflessness in people; children's needs and desires often come before those of the parents. And although you may not mind this at all, it is still important to not forget about each other.

Table 9.2 Strengths of Happy Versus Unhappy Couples regarding Parenting

| | PERCENTAGE IN AGREEMENT | |
| | HAPPY | UNHAPPY |
PARENTING ISSUE	COUPLES	COUPLES
1. I am satisfied with how childrearing is shared.	89%	36%
2. My partner focuses as much on our marriage as on the children.	63	32
3. We agree on discipline.	59	30
4. We agree on how to provide financially for the children.	60	38
5. Children do not create major problems in our marriage.	61	38

In fact, a strength of happy couples is that they are about twice as likely (63%) as unhappy couples (32%) to report that their partners give attention to the marriage as well as the child(ren). Taking time each day to share the day's events and to connect with each other is important. You need to be proactive in planning your time together. If your marriage is going to be satisfying, it cannot be left to chance. And your child(ren) will benefit from the effort you put into your marital relationship. You and your spouse are critical role models for your child(ren)'s prototype of how partners relate to each other.

Recognizing That Parenting Is a Team Effort

It's time for us to turn to each other, not on each other.

—Jesse Jackson

As Table 9.2 shows, satisfaction with how the responsibility of raising children is shared is the most significant issue distinguishing happy and unhappy couples. Happily married couples are more than twice as likely (63%) to be satisfied with how childrearing and parenting are shared than unhappily married couples (27%).

Co-parenting is simply a team approach to parenting. Co-parenting involves sharing all aspects of the child's growth and is based on the principle that the commitment and devotion of each parent is necessary to raise a well-adjusted child. Each parent has something unique to offer his or her children. Researchers have found that co-parenting improves both the marital relationship and the relationship between parent and child. Parenthood is much too important and much too time-consuming to be left up to one person.

Supporting Each Other

Researchers often find higher levels of marital satisfaction in child-free marriages than in marriages with children. However, this difference is not significant with parents who get along well and have a strong commitment to co-parenting.

Parenting is demanding, and one way to help each other and to show you care is through mutual support. One way to be supportive is through parenting together. Another way is to continue building on your marriage and your lives. For example, continue dating your partner. As a couple, you need to fight for time to be together.

It is important to maintain your friendship with your partner as well. In addition, you should share some of your everyday experiences with your children. Parents commonly ask their children about their day while neglecting to share their own stories. If you talk to your children about your friends, job, activities, dreams, and concerns, they will be more likely to share their lives with you. By making a conscious effort to maintain and create a happy marriage and personal life, you will be better parents.

Developing a Joint Plan on Discipline

Happily married couples are much more likely to agree on discipline than are unhappily married couples. Thus, it's important to discuss and develop a joint plan for discipline. It sounds so basic, but the fact is many couples disagree on how to discipline their child(ren).

Children quickly pick up on differences in parenting, and they may manipulate parents or direct their requests according to how they have learned each parent will respond. A simplistic but classic example illustrates this phenomenon. Suppose young Dylan asks his mother if he can have a cookie. His mother might respond, "I would like for you to wait until after dinner, since we will be eating soon and I want you to have room in your tummy for healthy food." Because Dylan is only 4 years old, he is not happy with his mother's reply to his request—he wants that cookie now. So he seeks out his father and asks him if he can have a cookie. Dylan's father did not hear the exchange between Mom and Dylan, and he tells Dylan that he can have a cookie.

What Dylan has learned is that if one parent says no, he merely needs to ask the other parent. The cookie itself is harmless, but the lesson Dylan learns can have more serious implications later in life and ultimately make it more difficult to parent him. Therefore, you should frequently discuss discipline and parenting style with your partner so that you can present a united front to your child(ren).

You will also need to adjust your parenting style and disciplinary procedures according to the age of your child(ren). It is important to have a consistent plan so that your child(ren) cannot play you and your spouse off against each other. If children sense dissension, they may use it to divide you and hurt themselves in the process.

Styles of Parenting

Differing ideas about how best to parent is an issue for about two-thirds of couples. Diana Baumrind (1991, 1995) has done considerable research on parenting styles and has identified four styles of parenting: democratic (authoritative), authoritarian, permissive, and rejecting. We added the uninvolved style, which was adapted from the Family Map (see Figure 9.1).

Democratic Parenting

In *democratic parenting*, parents establish clear rules and expectations and discuss them with the child. Although they acknowledge the child's perspective, they use both reason and power to enforce their standards. The democratic style is represented by the "balanced" type of system on the Family Map. Democratic families, therefore, tend to range from connected to cohesive on the cohesion dimension and from structured to flexible on the flexibility dimension.

Figure 9.1 Five Parenting Styles on the Family Map

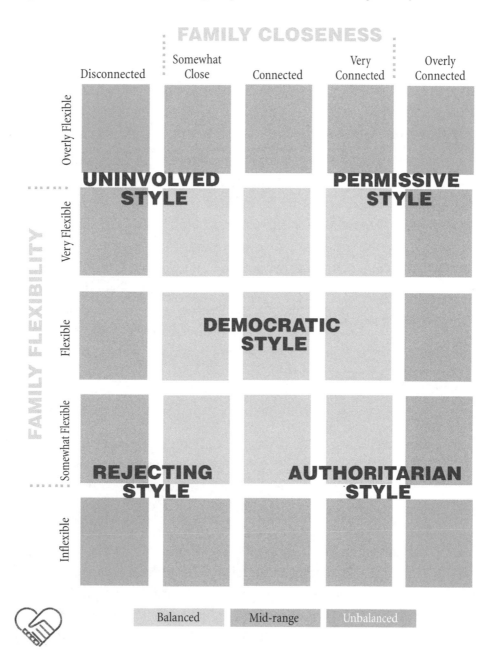

Considerable research on parenting has demonstrated that more balanced families have children who are more emotionally healthy and happy and are more successful in school and life (Kouneski, 1996). Children of authoritative-style parents exhibit what Baumrind describes as energetic-friendly behavior. These children are very self-reliant and cheerful, they cope well with stress, and they are achievement oriented.

Authoritarian Parenting

In *authoritarian parenting,* parents have more rigid rules and expectations and strictly enforce them. These parents expect and demand obedience from their children. The authoritarian style is located in the lower right quadrant of the Family Map, indicating a structured-to-rigid family system in terms of flexibility and a cohesive-to-enmeshed family system in terms of cohesion. As the authoritarian style becomes more intense, the family moves toward the unbalanced style called "rigidly enmeshed." This type of family system is particularly problematic for adolescents, who tend to rebel against it. In Baumrind's studies, children of authoritarian-style parents are often conflicted-irritable in behavior, they tend to be moody, unhappy, vulnerable to stress, and unfriendly.

Permissive Parenting

In *permission parenting,* parents let the child's preferences take priority over their ideals and rarely force the child to conform to their standards. The permissive style is located in the upper right quadrant of the Family Map, indicating families that are more flexible-to-chaotic on flexibility and more cohesive-to-enmeshed on cohesion. As the permissive style becomes more extreme, the family moves toward the "chaotic enmeshed" style. The chaotic enmeshed style is problematic for parenting because the constant change and forced togetherness is not healthy for children. Baumrind observed that children of permissive-style parents generally exhibit impulsive-aggressive behavior. These children are often rebellious, domineering, and low achievers.

Rejecting Parenting

In *rejecting parenting,* parents do not pay much attention to their child's needs and seldom have expectations regarding how the child should behave. The rejecting style is located in the lower left quadrant of the Family Map, indicating families that tend to range from structured to rigid in terms of flexibility and from connected to disengaged in terms of cohesion. As the rejecting style becomes more extreme, the family moves toward the "rigidly disengaged" style. This style makes it difficult for children to feel cared for, yet they are expected to behave because there are many rules. As a result, children from these homes are often immature and have psychological problems.

Uninvolved Parenting

In *uninvolved parenting,* parents often ignore the child, letting the child's preferences prevail as long as those preferences do not interfere with the parents' activities. The uninvolved style of parenting is located in the upper left quadrant of the Family Map, indicating a family that is connected-to-disengaged on cohesion and is flexible-to-chaotic on flexibility. As the uninvolved style becomes more extreme, it moves toward the "chaotic disengaged" pattern. This pattern is problematic for children because they are left on their own without emotional support and a lack of consistent rules and expectations. The uninvolved style of parenting is not often discussed in published research, but in many instances it is combined with the rejecting style. Children of uninvolved parents are often withdrawn loners and low achievers.

Table 9.3 summarizes the five parenting styles and children's consequent behavior for each.

Table 9.3 Parenting Styles and Children's Behavior

PARENTING STYLE	CHILDREN'S BEHAVIOR
Democratic	Energetic-friendly
	Self-reliant and cheerful
	Achievement oriented
Authoritarian	Unfriendly
	Conflicted and irritable
	Unhappy and unstable
Permissive	Impulsive and rebellious
	Low achieving
Rejecting	Immature
	Psychologically troubled
Uninvolved	Lonely and Withdrawn
	Low Achieving

Parenting as Peoplemaking

Virginia Satir (1972, 1988) coined the term "peoplemaking" as a euphemism for parenting. As a parent, you play many roles including nurse, storyteller, counselor, entertainer, encourager, organizer, nurturer, and mediator. Each role is different in action but equal in importance. And as a parent, you are both teacher and student. What a glorious privilege it is to be such an important person in the life of a child. The following poem describes the importance of focusing on peoplemaking rather than more external things.

One hundred years from now
It will not matter
What kind of car I drove,
What kind of house I lived in,
How much money I had in my bank account,
Nor what my clothes looked like.

But one hundred years from now
The world may be a little better
Because I was important
In the life of a child

—Anonymous

Couple Exercise 9.1
Planning a Weekly Family Conference

A family conference is a time for the family to connect and to reflect on recent family and personal experiences. Spending this time together helps family members feel supported and gives a new energy and sense of solidarity to the family system.

1. Be sure that everyone participates.

2. Establish a regular time and place—perhaps following a time the entire family is normally together, such as after dinner.

3. Encourage and share ideas. Do not criticize or critique.

4. Have each family member discuss the following three questions:

   a. What do you feel was the best thing that happened to you or happened within our family this week?

   b. What was the worst thing that happened to you within your family this week?

   c. For an issue that was brought up in step b, what could have been done differently?

Couple Exercise 9.2
Discussing Your Strengths and Growth Areas in Parenting

TAKING PARENTING QUIZ:

Each partner should take this Parenting Quiz and record your responses below.

IDENTIFY YOUR COUPLE STRENGTHS:

Strengths are the items where you both agree with each other. On items 1, 2 and 5, circle those items if you both agreed (response 4 or 5).

On items 3 and 4, circle the items if you both disagreed (response 1 or 2). *Circle the Strength items you identified.*

COUPLE DISCUSSION:

1. Discuss your Strengths and be proud of them.
2. Discuss the other items and decide how you can turn them into strengths.

Response Choices

1	2	3	4	5
Strongly Disagree	Disagree	Undecided	Agree	Strongly Agree

	PARTNER 1	PARTNER 2
1. The father is actively involved in childrearing and parenting.	_____	_____
2. We're satisfied with how we discipline our child(ren).	_____	_____
3. Parenting is stressful on our marriage.	_____	_____
4. We give more attention to our children than our marriage.	_____	_____
5. We are satisfied with how we share parenting.	_____	_____

Scoring of the Quiz

1. Individually take the quiz.

2. Score the quiz as follows:
   a. Total your points for items 1, 2, and 5.   _____
   b. Add 12 to total of a.   __+12__
   c. Total points for items 3 and 4.   _____
   d. Subtract c from b.   _____

   PARTNER 1:_____   PARTNER 2: _____

3. Interpreting your score: Range = 5–25

   21–25 = You have many strengths in parenting.
   15–20 = Your parenting is generally good, but there are some ways it could
           be improved.
   11–14 = Your parenting is good in some ways but also needs some
           improvement.
    5–10 = Your co-parenting needs improvement.

4. After you have both taken and scored the Quiz, compare how you perceive
   your relationship regarding children and parenting.

Suggestions for Improving Your Parenting

1. Give attention to your marriage as well as to your children.

2. Discuss discipline styles and expectations with your partner.

3. Support each other in all aspects of parenting.

4. Be consistent and cooperative as a parenting team.

**Turn your stumbling blocks
into stepping stones!**

Chapter Ten

Personal, Couple, and Family Goals

The most powerful weapon on earth
is the human soul on fire.

—Marshall Ferdinand Foch (1851–1929)

Goal Quiz

How satisfied are you with your goals—personally, as a couple, and as a family?

You can take this Goal Quiz alone and see how you score individually using the format and scoring at the end of chapter.

Encourage your partner to also take the Goal Quiz so you can identify your strengths and issues regarding your goals. Instructions for scoring and discussing the Quiz are described at the end of chapter in Couple Exercise 10.3.

Response Choices

1	2	3	4	5
Strongly Disagree	Disagree	Undecided	Agree	Strongly Agree

1. We share common couple and family goals.

2. My partner is supportive of my personal goals.

3. Our personal and family goals are not clearly defined.

4. We are able to accomplish most of our goals.

5. We have clear goals for our couple relationship.

What Do You Hope For?

*The very least you can do in your life is to figure out
what you hope for. And the most you can do is live inside that hope.
Not admire it from a distance but live right in it, under its roof.*

—Barbara Kingsolver

There is an old saying that defines three things we need in life: something to do, something to love, and something to hope for. We all need hopes and dreams for the future. If we do not have a goal, we may not feel motivated to keep going through tough times. Goals provide direction and give hope for the future. It is valuable for couples to review their personal, couple, and family goals. Discussing and sharing goals facilitates closeness, emotional bonding, and goal achievement. Our goals are an expression of who we are, so they touch on a myriad of deeply personal issues and feelings.

Goals we set for ourselves are directly influenced by what we believe we can and cannot achieve. This chapter is written in a slightly different style than the previous nine chapters. You will also notice that there are more quotations and excerpts from other writings. This is because there is so much that we can learn from one another, and the area of goals in particular highlights people's similarities in terms of their desires, fears, hopes, and joys.

Common Stumbling Blocks to Achieving Goals

Obstacles don't have to stop you. If you run into a wall, don't turn around and give up. Figure out how to climb it, go through it, or work around it.

—Michael Jordan

Defining and attaining goals is not always easy, but it is not supposed to be. We have to expect obstacles, delays, and disappointments. But the challenges associated with setting and achieving goals make the rewards that much more fulfilling.

Lack of Awareness of Each Other's Goals

You can make it, but it's easier if you don't have to do it alone.

—Betty Ford

Sometimes, one partner's lack of awareness of the other's goals is interpreted as a lack of support. For example, you might be trying to lose weight and feel that your partner is sabotaging your diet by eating tempting foods in front of you. But if you talk with your partner about your goals and desires—in this case, to lose weight—he or she will be better able to encourage and support you, and vice versa. Studies have shown that couple support is one of the more powerful ways of helping partners change negative health behaviors or recover from illness.

Personal Versus Family Goals

Sometimes, one partner's personal goal may interfere with a family goal. For example, the wife may want to go back to work full-time, which means she won't be as available to care for the children, prepare meals, and do household chores. Or one partner may want to go back to school while the other wants to start saving for children's college. These two goals are potentially very conflicting and can cause tension in the family and couple relationship.

Conflicting Goals in Couples

Having different goals can cause problems in your marriage, particularly if the goals differ for your family and couple relationships. For example, you may be striving to earn more money while your partner is more interested in spending time with the children or you. This means you may not end up doing much together because of your different goals. If this is the case, you and your partner need to discuss the differences and come to some resolution. In Couple Exercise 10.1, you will have an opportunity to prioritize your goals. Once you each do this, you can determine what is most important to you and what you are willing to compromise on. You can still support and encourage each other even if your goals differ.

Negative Thinking

It is not your actual circumstances that cause your emotions, but your thoughts or attitudes about those circumstances. And you have total control over your thoughts and attitudes. As Henry Ford wittily observed, *"Whether you think you can or think you can't, you are right."* So, although you cannot control your emotions, you can learn to choose the thoughts that produce them.

Many people make the mistake of telling themselves they can't do something. With a "can't" attitude, you simply set yourself up for failure—failure that usually has nothing to do with ability and everything to do with willingness. "Can't" almost always means "won't." From now on, when the word "can't" seeps into your mind, think about it as an acronym:

<u>C</u>an
<u>A</u>fter
<u>N</u>umerous
<u>T</u>ries

When you change your thinking, you can change your life. Here's how:
When you change your thinking, you change your beliefs,
When you change your beliefs, you change your expectations,
When you change your expectations, you change your attitude,
When you change your attitude, you change your behavior,
When you change your behavior, you change your performance,
When you change your performance, you change your life.

—Anonymous

Procrastination

Woody Allen once said, *"Most of life is just about showing up."* Although this sounds simplistic, if you think about it, you'll realize that it makes sense. As a working person, the most difficult part of your day is likely right after waking, when you have to motivate yourself to actually get out of bed and get ready to go to work.

As a runner who has trained for and run a marathon, I can testify that the hardest part of those training runs was feeling motivated enough to put on my running shoes. Once I was running, I was happy to be doing it. And afterwards, I usually felt exhilarated, fulfilled and renewed. We all know that half of the battle is simply getting started. Once you start something, you will be into it. Don't hold back. Now is the most important time in your life. What are you waiting for?

It takes a tremendous amount of energy to procrastinate. As William James pointed out, *"There's nothing as fatiguing as holding on to an uncompleted task."* Use that energy—don't waste it.

Suggestions for Achieving Goals

Many of us are afraid to follow our passions, to pursue what
we want most because it means taking risks and even facing failure.
But to pursue your passion with all your heart and soul is success in itself.
The greatest failure is to have never really tried.

—Robyn Allan

Define and Prioritize Goals

Often we do not take time to reflect on and think about what our goals are. Rather, we tend to follow routines. It is easy merely to go through each day and not to challenge ourselves to try new things. But you need to be more proactive than reactive in terms of your goals; you need focus and direction. Defining your goals enables you to envision and strive toward them. It also helps you gain a sense of progress as you move toward these goals. In Couple Exercise 10.1, you will have the chance to list and prioritize your goals.

Once you have determined what it is you want, you need to prioritize goals and examine the aspects of your life that may be affected. What is most important to you? On what are you not willing to compromise? For example, if you have a goal of saving for a family vacation, and you have the option of working overtime to earn extra money, you may need to evaluate how much time you will spend away from your family working overtime. If you determine that the cost of less family time for several months is too high a price to pay, then you may need to consider other ways of saving money.

Visualize Goals

Whatever you can do or dream you can do, you can.
Boldness has a genius magic and power to it.

—Johann Goethe (1749–1842)

It is human nature for us to become what we think we are. For example, if you think of yourself as being lazy, you will act lazy; if you think of yourself as being friendly, you will tend to act friendly. Once you define your goals, you need to focus on and visualize them. Albert Einstein, one of the master problem solvers of all time, knew the value of visualization: *"Imagination is more important than knowledge. Your imagination is the preview to life's coming attraction."*

Create a mental picture of your goal in action. You know what it is you want to do. You want to vacation in Australia? Imagine yourself exploring the Great Barrier Reef, climbing Ayers Rock, and eating shrimp off the "barbie." You want to strengthen your relationship with your partner? Imagine taking a class together, having enjoyable conversations, and laughing out loud as you walk hand in hand. You want more education? Imagine yourself sitting in a classroom learning or sitting in the library reading something that stimulates, challenges and excites you. You want to fit into all the clothes in your closet again? Visualize yourself in the physical condition that you desire. Hold that thought in your mind, and do what you need to do every day to bring yourself one day closer to your goals.

"Fall Down Seven Times, Get Up Eight"

*Some of the best lessons we ever learn we learn from our mistakes
and failures. The error of the past is the wisdom of the future.*

—Tryon Edwards

Have you ever noticed that the lives of people who have achieved their dreams are filled with numerous past "failures"? Why is that? They do not let disappointments define themselves. These people are persistent; they persevere. They continue trying because they know that "mistakes" are simply a part of the journey to success. For example, if you have ever watched babies learning to walk, you will have noticed that they continuously pull themselves up, fall down, pull themselves up again, eventually take a step or two, fall down, and so on. They are living what is expressed in the Japanese proverb "Fall down seven times, get up eight."

The noted sports psychologist and motivational speaker Dr. Rob Gilbert often points out, "Winners lose more than losers lose." What exactly does this mean? On one of his "Success Hotline" messages, he offers the following Autobiography of a Loser? *"I have missed more than 9,000 shots in my career. I have lost almost 300 games. On twenty-six occasions I had to take the game-winning shot and I missed. And I failed over and over and over again in my life—that is precisely why I succeed."* These are the words of Michael Jordan, possibly the greatest basketball player of all time. So, winners lose more than losers lose because winners try more than losers.

As the great actress Mary Pickford observed: *"Today is a new day. You will get out of it just what you put into it. If you have made mistakes, there is always another chance for you. And supposing you have tried and failed again and again, you may have a fresh start any moment you choose, for this thing that we call 'failure' is not the falling down, but the staying down."*

Don't be afraid to make mistakes. Mistakes give you an opportunity to examine behaviors and habits and to understand the connection between new actions and new outcomes. To stop making mistakes is to also stop learning, growing, and improving. People who aren't making mistakes are on a detour from the road to success and improvement, and that is a bigger mistake.

Identify Steps for Achieving Goals

If you want to make progress, you have to progress through your problems.
—Rob Gilbert, Ph.D.

Instead of thinking in terms of the "big picture," break your goal down into small, bite-size chunks. If you wanted to run a marathon, you wouldn't just go out and run one. You might start out jogging a mile or two at a time, and then gradually increase your distance.

Similarly, if you want to improve your relationship with your partner, remember that it is the small things you do that make a big difference in the long run. Begin by consciously complimenting your partner at least one additional time each day. Show that you care by making eye contact and really listening. Be generous with hugs, kisses, and caresses. Send a no-occasion card to your home or your partner's workplace. Or simply pay attention to something your partner enjoys and surprise him or her with it.

Think about and work toward your goal every day. Think of the small steps you can take to bring you closer to your goal. Ask yourself, "Is what I'm doing right now getting me closer to my goal?" "Are these cookies getting me closer to my goal of weight loss?" "Are my criticisms of my spouse bringing me closer to my goal of a fulfilling marriage?" "Is this the best use of my time right now?"

Achieving Goals

In organizing and prioritizing goals, one of the first steps is to make certain the goal is in alignment with your principles and values and those of others in your life. Ask yourself, "Will this goal cause me to neglect the important relationships in my life?" Remember: the way you spend your time is a reflection of your priorities.

In the couple exercises that follows, you will have a chance to define personal, couple, and family goals. Developing goals for all three areas will help you balance health, family, professional, couple, and personal issues. Writing down your goals is a great way to clarify and integrate what's in your conscious mind and your subconscious. Having goals in writing keeps them clearly before you both visually and mentally.

Remember, you need to keep taking "baby steps" toward your goal. Work on your goal together as a team.

> *Coming together is a beginning;*
> *Keeping together is progress;*
> *Working together is success.*
>
> —Anonymous

Couple Exercise 10.1
Defining Personal, Couple, and Family Goals

Clarify and define your personal, couple, and family goals for the next few years. Then share them with your partner. Remember your goals should be realistic and clearly stated. These goals also should be attainable within one to five years.

Partner 1 Goals

Personal Goals

1. _____

2. _____

3. _____

Couple Goals

1. _____

2. _____

3. _____

Family Goals

1. _____

2. _____

3. _____

Partner 2 Goals

Personal Goals

1. _____

2. _____

3. _____

Couple Goals

1. _____

2. _____

3. _____

Family Goals

1. _____

2. _____

3. _____

Couple Exercise 10.2
Developing A Couple Action Plan

Once you have identified personal, couple, and family goals, we encourage you to choose one of the three areas and develop an action plan based on the CHANGE Model. The six letters in CHANGE indicate an important step in achieving your goal. An example of how the CHANGE Model can be used follows each step.

COMMIT YOURSELF TO A SPECIFIC GOAL.

We will increase closeness in our marriage by spending 15 minutes each day focusing on the positive aspects of our relationship. We will try also to have a date with each other one evening a week.

HABITS—BREAK OLD ONES AND START NEW ONES.

We will set up the new routine so that the 15 minutes falls after the evening meal each night. The evening out will usually be on Wednesday night. We'll rotate on who chooses what to do on the evening out.

ACTION—TAKE ONE STEP AT A TIME.

During our 15 minutes of sharing, we will each talk about our day and our feelings about each other.

NEVER GIVE UP; LAPSES MIGHT OCCUR.

We realize that some days we won't be able to talk for 15 minutes about our relationship and that we won't be able to have an evening out every week, but we will do our best to stick to the plan.

GOAL-ORIENTED—FOCUS ON THE POSITIVE.

After our sharing, we will praise each other for taking the time and effort to connect with each other.

EVALUATE PROGRESS AND REWARD EACH OTHER.

Each Sunday night, we will review the week and see how well we've done. If we have achieved our goal, we will feel pleased, and this will probably make us feel closer. If we are able to stick to this plan for six months, the final reward will be a weekend trip away together to celebrate!

Creating Your Action Plan

Use this as a worksheet to complete your Personal, Couple, or Family Action Plan.

COMMIT YOURSELVES TO A SPECIFIC GOAL.
Describe your specific goal.

HABITS: BREAK OLD ONES AND START NEW ONES.
Old Habits:

New Plan:

ACTION: TAKE ONE STEP AT A TIME.
Indicate steps in plan.

NEVER GIVE UP; LAPSES MIGHT OCCUR.
How will you handle lapses?

GOAL ORIENTED: FOCUS ON THE POSITIVE.
When will you praise each other?

EVALUATE YOUR PROGRESS AND REWARD EACH OTHER.
When will you review your progress?

How will you reward each other?

Couple Exercise 10.3
Discussing Your Strengths and Growth Areas regarding Your Goals

TAKING GOALS QUIZ:

Each partner should take this Goals Quiz and record your responses below.

IDENTIFY YOUR COUPLE STRENGTHS:

Strengths are the items where you both agree with each other. On items 1, 2 4 and 5, circle those items if you both agreed (response 4 or 5). On item 3, circle it if you both disagreed (response 1 or 2). *Circle the Strength items you identified.*

COUPLE DISCUSSION:

1. Discuss your strengths and be proud of them.
2. Discuss the other items and decide how you can turn them into strengths.

Response Choices

1	2	3	4	5
Strongly Disagree	Disagree	Undecided	Agree	Strongly Agree

	PARTNER 1	PARTNER 2
1. We share common couple and family goals.	_____	_____
2. My partner is supportive of my personal goals.	_____	_____
3. Our personal and family goals are not clearly defined.	_____	_____
4. We are able to accomplish most of our goals.	_____	_____
5. We have clear goals for our couple relationship.	_____	_____

▬▬▬▬▬▬ Scoring of the Quiz ▬▬▬▬▬▬

1. Individually take the quiz.

2. Score the quiz as follows:
   a. Total your points for items 1, 2, 4, and 5. _____
   b. Add 6 to total of a. ___+6__
   c. Total points for item 3. _____
   d. Subtract c from b. _____

   PARTNER 1:_____   PARTNER 2: _____

3. Interpreting your score: Range = 5–25

   21–25 = You have very compatible goals and an easy time in
           accomplishing them.
   15–20 = You have compatible goals and a relatively easy time
           accomplishing them.
   11–14 = You have somewhat similar goals and are sometimes able to
           achieve them.
   5–10 = You have different goals and difficulty accomplishing them.

4. After you have both taken and scored the Quiz, compare how you perceive
   your relationship regarding goals.

Suggestions for Achieving Your Goals

1. Decide exactly what you want. Define and share with your partner your personal, couple, and family goals.

2. Discuss with each other steps you can take to make your goals a reality.

3. Start immediately. Use the CHANGE Model. Make the decision—day by day, to commit to the goal.

4. Encourage and support each other. Do not let setbacks discourage you. Recognize the valuable feedback that failure provides.

5. Never, ever give up.

Turn your stumbling blocks into stepping stones!

References and Resources

Albrecht, S. (1979). Correlates of marital happiness among the remarried. *Journal of Marriage and the Family, 41* (4), 858-867.

Altura, J. (1974). Poem. In *J. Gillies, My needs, your needs.* New York: Doubleday.

Aron, A. & Aron, E. (1991). Love and sexuality. In K. McKinney & S. Sprecher (Eds.), *Sexuality in close relationships.* Hillsdale, NJ: Erlbaum.

Arond, M., & Pauker, S.L. (1987). *The first year of marriage.* New York: Warner Books.

Burkett, L. (1993). *Complete financial guide for couples.* Wheaton, IL: Victor Books.

Baumrind, D. (1995). *Child maltreatment and optimal care-giving in social contexts.* New York: Garland.

Baumrind, D. (1991). The influence of parenting style on adolescent competence and substance abuse. *Journal of Early Adolescence, 11,* (1), 56-95.

Blumstein, P.W., & Schwartz, P. (1983). *American couples.* New York: Morrow.

Bock, E.W., & Radelt, M.L. (1988). The marital integration of religious independents: A reevaluation of its significance. *Review of Religious Research, 29,* 228-241.

Brooks, J. (1998). *Parenting.* Mountain View, CA: Mayfield.

Buechner, F. (1993). *Wishful thinking: A seeker's ABC.* San Francisco: Harper.

Burkett, L. (1993). *Complete financial guide for couples.* Wheaton, IL: Victor Books.

DeMaria, R.M. (1998). *A national survey of married couples who participate in marriage enrichment.* Unpublished dissertation, Bryn Mawr College, School of Social Work, Philadelphia.

Derlega, V., Metts, S., Petronio, S., & Margulis, S. (1993). *Self-disclosure.* Newbury Park, CA: Sage.

Dyer, P., & Dyer, G. (1990). *Growing Together.* Minneapolis: Life Innovations.

Fowers, B.J., Montel, K.H., & Olson, D.H. (1996). Predicting marital success for premarital couple types based on PREPARE. *Journal of Marital and Family Therapy. 12* (4), 403-413.

Fowers, B.J., & Olson, D.H. (1992). Four types of premarital couples: An empirical typology based on PREPARE. *Journal of Family Psychology, 6* (1), 10-21.

Gibran, K. (1976). *The Prophet.* New York: Knopf. (Original work published in 1923).

Gilbert, R. (1997). *More of the best of Bits & Pieces.* Fairfield, NJ: The Economics Press.

Gottmann, J. (1994). *Why marriages succeed or fail.* New York: Simon & Schuster.

Hayden, R.L., (1999). *For richer, not poorer: the money book for couples.* Deerfield Beach, FL: Health Communications.

Hochschild, A.R. (1989). *The second shift.* New York: Viking.

Hovfoll, S. & Hovfoll, I. (1994). *Work won't love you back.* New York: Freeman.

Kersey, C. (1998). *Unstoppable: 45 powerful stores of perseverance and triumph from people just like you.* Naperville, IL: Sourcebooks.

Kouneski, E.F. (1996). *Fatherhood today.* Unpublished article, University of Minnesota, Family Social Science, St. Paul.

Lenehan, A.F. (1994). *The best of Bits & Pieces.* Fairfield, NJ: The Economics Press.

Lerner, H.G. (1985). *The dance of anger.* New York: Harper & Row.

Lips, H. (1997). *Sex and gender* (3d ed.). Mountain View, CA: Mayfield.

Mahoney, A., Pargament, T.J., Swank, A.B., Scott, E., Emery, E., & Rye, M. (1999). Marriage and the spiritual realm: The role of proximal and distal religious constructs in marital functioning. *Journal of Family Psychology, 13* (3), 321-338.

Markman, H., Stanley, S. & Blumberg, S.L. (1994). *Fighting for your marriage.* San Francisco, CA: Jossey-Bass.

Martindale, J. & Moses, M. (1994). *52 simple ways to manage your money.* Naperville, IL: Sourcebooks.

Masters, W.H., Johnson, V., & Kolodny, R.C., (1988). *Masters & Johnson on sex and human loving.* Boston: Little Brown.

Minirth, F. & M.A., Newman, B. & D., & Hemfelt, R. & S. (1993). *Renewing love: Your handbook for rekindling intimacy.* Nashville, TN: Nelson.

Oliver, G., & Wright, N. (1992). *When anger hits home: Taking care of your anger without taking it out on your family.* Chicago: Moody Press.

Olson, D.H. (1996). Clinical assessment and treatment using the Circumplex Model. In F.W. Kaslow (Ed.), *Handbook in relational diagnosis* (pp. 59-80). New York: Wiley.

Olson, D.H., DeFrain, J. & Olson, A. (1999). *Building relationships: Developing skills for life.* Minneapolis, MN: Life Innovations.

Olson, D.H. & DeFrain, J. (2000). *Marriage and the family: Diversity and strengths* (3rd ed.). Mountain View, CA: Mayfield.

Perls, F. (1969). Gestalt therapy verbatim (p. 4). Lafayette, CA: Real People Press.

Peterson, K.S. (1992, March 12). Adults should know status of parents. *USA Today.* p. 1D.

Pietropinto, A. & Simenauer, J. (1979). *Husbands and wives: A nationwide survey of marriage.* New York: Times Books.

Pybrum, S. (1996). *Money and marriage: Making it work together.* Santa Barbara, CA: Abundance.

Riesenberg, M. (1997). *How to stop whining and start winning: A guide to goal setting and time management.* Dubuque, IA: Kendall-Hunt.

Satir, V. (1988). *The new peoplemaking.* Palo Alto, CA: Science and Behavior Books.

Schneidervin, J. (1996). *Deepening love for marital happiness.* Milwaukee, WI: Northwestern.

Sprecher, S. & McKinney, K. (1993). *Sexuality.* Newbury Park, CA: Sage.

Thorton, J. (1997). *Chore wars: How households can share the work and keep the peace.* Berkeley, CA: Conari Press.

Waite, L. (1995). "Does marriage matter?" *Demography, 32* (4), 483-507.

Waite, L., & Gallagher, M. (2000). *The case for marriage.* Cambridge: Harvard University Press.

Walsh, F. (1999). *Spiritual resources in family therapy.* New York: Guilford Press.

Whisman, M.A., Dixon, A.E., & Johnson, B. (1998). Therapists' perspectives of couple problems and treatment issues in couple therapy. *Journal of Family Psychology, 11* (3), 361-366.

National Sample of Married Couples:

Demographic Information

Our national sample consisted of 21,501 married couples who took the ENRICH couple inventory during 1998 and 1999. The couples took the inventory as part of either couple enrichment or couple therapy. It was administered by a professional counselor or clergyperson who had been trained to use the PREPARE/ENRICH inventories.

From this total sample of 21,501 married couples, the most happily married couples (n = 5,153) and the most unhappily married couples (n = 5,127) were used for some of the analysis. The level of marital happiness was assessed, based on the marital satisfaction scale from ENRICH. Happily married couples had a positive couple agreement (PCA) score on ENRICH of 70%-100%, and the unhappily married couples had a PCA score of 0-40%. High PCA scores generally mean that both partners are happy, and low PCA scores generally indicate that both partners are unhappy. Couples with a PCA score of 50%-60% were excluded from the happy or unhappy group since, typically, one partner was considerably more happy than the other partner.

States Represented in the Sample

The sample of ENRICH couples was taken from all fifty states (see Table 1). The largest percentage of the sample came from California (10.2%), Minnesota (8.4%), and Texas (8.0%). A significant percentage also came from Michigan (5.1%), Illinois (5.0%), Pennsylvania, and Ohio (3.8%). Three more states had at least 3% of the sample, including Wisconsin (3.5%), Florida (3.3%), and Washington (3.2%). Eight states had between 2–3% of the sample, including New York, Oregon, Iowa, Indiana, North Carolina, Colorado, Georgia, and Virginia. Six more states had between 1.5% and 2.0% of the sample, including Kansas, Tennessee, Maryland, Missouri, New Jersey, and North Dakota. The other 26 states contained a smaller percentage of the sample, anywhere from 0.2% to 1.4%.

Table I: ENRICH Sample—Top 25 States

California	10.2%	Indiana	2.3%
Minnesota	8.4	North Carolina	2.2
Texas	8.0	Colorado	2.0
Michigan	5.1	Georgia	2.0
Illinois	5.0	Virginia	2.0
Pennsylvania	4.0	Kansas	1.9
Ohio	3.8	Tennessee	1.8
Wisconsin	3.5	Maryland	1.7
Florida	3.3	Missouri	1.7
Washington	3.2	New Jersey	1.6
New York	2.7	North Dakota	1.5
Oregon	2.5	Nebraska	<u>1.4</u>
Iowa	2.3		
		Subtotal	84.1%
	25 states with less than 1.4%		<u>15.9%</u>
		Total	100%

Level of Marital Satisfaction

For the total sample of 21,501 married couples, 60% reported that they were satisfied or very satisfied with their marriage, 12% reported that they were neutral, and 28% reported that they were dissatisfied or very dissatisfied.

Happy and unhappy couples differed greatly in terms of their marital satisfaction. The greatest disparity between happy and unhappy couples was in the number of happy couples who were satisfied or very satisfied with their marriage (98%) and the number of unhappy couples who were satisfied or very satisfied with their marriage (33.9%). Less than 2% of the happy couples were neutral, dissatisfied, or very dissatisfied while 66% of the unhappy couples were neutral, dissatisfied, or very dissatisfied.

LEVEL OF MARITAL SATISFACTION	TOTAL SAMPLE	HAPPY MARRIAGES	UNHAPPY MARRIAGES
Very dissatisfied	8.3%	0%	12.5%
Dissatisfied	20.0	0	34.7
Neutral	12.0	2.0	19.0
Satisfied	27.6	16.5	27.4
Very satisfied	32.3	81.5	6.5

Perceived Partners' Marital Satisfaction

The percentages for marital satisfaction were very similar. In terms of partners' marital satisfaction for the overall sample, 31% reported that their partner was dissatisfied or very dissatisfied with their marriage, 11% responded that their partner was neutral, and 58% said that their partner was satisfied or very satisfied.

As expected, when individuals described their partners' marital satisfaction, it was much greater in happy couples than unhappy couples. While 98% of happy couples partners reported they were satisfied or very satisfied; only 32.7% of the unhappy couples reported that they were satisfied or very satisfied. While none of happy couples reported their partner as neutral, dissatisfied, or very dissatisfied, 67.3% of unhappy couples reported that their partner was neutral, dissatisfied, or very dissatisfied.

PERCEIVED PARTNER'S MARITAL SATISFACTION	TOTAL SAMPLE	HAPPY MARRIAGES	UNHAPPY MARRIAGES
Very dissatisfied	10.5%	0%	15.1%
Dissatisfied	20.5	0	35.6
Neutral	11.0	6.0	16.6
Satisfied	29.9	20.4	27.1
Very satisfied	28.2	73.6	5.6

Age Distribution

The national survey included a wide range of age groups with the average age being about 35 years for males and 32 years for females. Overall, 30% of the couples were 30 years of age or younger while about 38% of the couples ranged from 31 to 40 years old. Couples 41 or older represented 32% of the total sample. There were no significant differences in the ages of the happy and unhappy couples.

Years of Age	Total Sample	Happy Marriages	Unhappy Marriages
25 or younger	12.6%	11.7%	12.4%
26–30	17.5	15.8	18.0
31–35	19.8	18.6	21.8
36–40	18.4	17.0	19.3
41 or older	31.5	36.8	28.3

Years Married

A majority of the couples (42 %) were married five years or less, 35% were married for six to fifteen years, and 23% were married sixteen years or more. There were no significant differences between happy and unhappy couples in terms of years married.

Years Married	Total Sample	Happy Marriages	Unhappy Marriages
0–5	42.5%	43.8%	41.5%
6–10	20.7	17.3	22.5
11–15	13.9	11.8	15.5
16 or more	22.8	27.2	20.3

Education

For the total sample, about 18% had completed high school or had some high school education. Over one-third (36 %) had some college or technical college, and about one-quarter (23.5%) had a four-year college degree. One-fifth (21.5%) had a graduate or professional degree.

The happy couples were slightly more educated than the unhappy couples, having higher percentages in number of four-year college graduates (happy 26.3% versus unhappy 20.1%) and number of individuals attending graduate or professional schools (happy 26.5% versus unhappy 17.3%).

EDUCATION COMPLETED	TOTAL SAMPLE	HAPPY MARRIAGES	UNHAPPY MARRIAGES
Graduate/professional	21.5%	26.5%	17.3%
4-year college	23.5	26.3	20.1
Some college/technical	36.0	30.5	40.5
High school or less	17.5	16.8	22.2

Employment

Two-thirds (68%) of the sample were employed full-time while 13% had part-time jobs. Another 19% were either unemployed or had both full and part-time jobs. No significant differences were found in this area between happy and unhappy couples.

EMPLOYMENT	TOTAL SAMPLE	HAPPY MARRIAGES	UNHAPPY MARRIAGES
Full-time	67.6%	70.1%	66.5%
Part-time	13.3	13.0	13.3
Other	19.0	16.9	20.2

Occupation

The individuals in this sample held a number of different occupations. About one-fifth (21.7 %) were in either clerical, sales, or technical work. Another one-fifth (18.6%) were managers, teachers, or nurses. A small percentage were in other occupations including self-employed (10.0%); executive, doctor, or lawyer (7.3%); factory, laborer, or wait staff (6.7%), and trades or farmer (6.2%). About 30% held other various occupations. There were no significant occupational differences between happy and unhappy couples.

OCCUPATION	TOTAL SAMPLE	HAPPY MARRIAGES	UNHAPPY MARRIAGES
Clerical/sales/technical	21.7%	20.2%	22.6%
Executive/doctor/lawyer	7.3	9.1	5.4
Factory/laborer/wait staff	6.7	6.2	7.8
Manager/teacher/nurse	18.6	21.0	16.7
Self-employed	10.0	8.9	11.1
Trades/farmer	6.2	5.3	7.5
Other	29.7	29.3	29.0

Income

In terms of annual income, just under half (48%) of the sample earned $29,999 or less, while about 28% earned between $30,000 and $49,999. About one-quarter (23.6%) earned $50,000 or more per year. There were no significant differences between happy and unhappy couples in this area.

INCOME	TOTAL SAMPLE	HAPPY MARRIAGES	UNHAPPY MARRIAGES
$19,999 or less	28.3%	25.2%	31.0%
$20,000–$29,999	20.2	19.9	21.3
$30,000–$39,999	16.7	16.1	16.7
$40,000–$49,999	11.4	11.8	11.2
$50,000–$74,999	13.6	15.0	12.3
$75,000 or more	10.0	12.1	7.6

Religious Orientation

In religious orientation, the majority of the sample (54%) was Protestant. About 16% were Catholic, and 27.9% were of other religions. There was a difference between happy and unhappy couples in that more unhappy couples listed "Other" as their religion.

RELIGION	TOTAL SAMPLE	HAPPY MARRIAGES	UNHAPPY MARRIAGES
Catholic	16.0%	23.3%	11.3%
Protestant	54.8	56.0	53.1
Other	27.9	19.4	34.6

Ethnic Background

The vast majority of the sample (85.2%) was Caucasian, while a small percentage was African American (5.7%), Hispanic/Latino (3.7%), or other races (5.6%). The differences between happy and unhappy couples were insignificant.

ETHNICITY	TOTAL SAMPLE	HAPPY MARRIAGES	UNHAPPY MARRIAGES
African American	5.7%	4.9%	5.5%
Caucasian	85.2	87.4	85.0
Hispanic/Latino	3.7	3.0	4.1
Other	5.6	4.8	5.4

Residence

Just under one quarter of the sample lived in rural areas (23.4%), in towns (22.1%), or in large cities (24.3%). About 30% of the sample lived in small cities. No significant differences were found between happy and unhappy couples in this area.

RESIDENCE	TOTAL SAMPLE	HAPPY MARRIAGES	UNHAPPY MARRIAGES
Rural	23.4%	22.8%	25.1%
Town	22.1	20.7	24.9
Small city	30.3	30.6	28.1
Large city	24.3	26.1	22.0

Parents' Marital Status

In terms of their parents' marital status, almost half of the sample (47.2%) were married, and close to a quarter (23.2%) were remarried. About 14% of the parents were single, with their partner deceased, and 8.5% had parents who were separated or divorced. About 7% had parents who were both deceased. The percentages for happy and unhappy couples were similar in this area.

PARENT'S MARITAL STATUS	TOTAL SAMPLE	HAPPY MARRIAGES	UNHAPPY MARRIAGES
Married	47.2%	47.7%	44.7%
Remarried	23.2	21.7	26.0
Separated/divorced	8.5	7.5	10.0
Single, partner deceased	14.4	16.0	13.9
Both parents deceased	6.9	9.3	5.4

Birth Position

In terms of birth position, 37% of the sample were born first, 28% were born second, 17% were born third, and 18% were born fourth or fifth. Happy and unhappy couples were generally similar in birth order.

BIRTH POSITION	TOTAL SAMPLE	HAPPY MARRIAGES	UNHAPPY MARRIAGES
First	37.1%	36.6%	36.6%
Second	27.7	27.3	27.4
Third	17.2	16.8	17.5
Fourth or fifth	18.1	19.3	18.6

Number of Children in Family

About one-quarter of the sample lived in families with two children (26%) or with three children (27%). The average number of children was 3.2 for all three groups. Close to 18% of the couples lived in families with four children, and one-fifth (21.7%) lived in families with five children. Eight percent of the sample were from families with one child. Happy and unhappy couples were very similar regarding number of children.

CHILDREN IN FAMILY	TOTAL SAMPLE	HAPPY MARRIAGES	UNHAPPY MARRIAGES
One	8.0%	6.9%	8.1%
Two	25.7	25.4	25.5
Three	26.7	26.0	26.3
Four	17.9	18.1	18.2
Five	21.7	23.5	22.0

Children

For the total sample, one-quarter (24.8%) of the couples had no children, 47.7% had one to two children, and 27% had three or more children. The happy and unhappy couples differed somewhat in how many children they had, with 32% of the happy couples having no children and 18.5% of the unhappy couples having no children. Forty-two percent of the happy couples had one to two children while 52% of the unhappy couples had one to two children. Twenty-six percent of the happy couples had three or more children while 30% of the unhappy couples had three or more children.

NUMBER OF CHILDREN	TOTAL SAMPLE	HAPPY MARRIAGES	UNHAPPY MARRIAGES
None	24.8%	32.0%	18.5%
One	17.9	15.7	19.5
Two	29.8	25.9	32.3
Three	16.9	15.7	18.3
Four or more	10.6	10.7	11.5

Parents' Alcohol and Drug Use

Almost 70% of the total sample had parents who seldom or never used alcohol or drugs. About 11% of the couples had parents who sometimes used alcohol or drugs, and 19.0% had parents who often or very often used alcohol and drugs.

Happy and unhappy couples differed somewhat in terms of their parents' alcohol and drug use. Over three-quarters (77.1%) of the happy couples had parents who seldom or never used alcohol or drugs while about two-thirds (65.1%) of the unhappy couples had parents who seldom or never used alcohol or drugs. Ten percent of the happy couples and 12.5% of the unhappy couples had parents who sometimes used alcohol or drugs. Compared with happy couples (13.4%), a higher percentage of unhappy couples (22.5%) had parents who often or very often used alcohol or drugs.

PARENTS' DRUG USE	TOTAL SAMPLE	HAPPY MARRIAGES	UNHAPPY MARRIAGES
Never	60.9%	68.2%	56.3%
Seldom	8.7	8.9	8.8
Sometimes	11.4	9.9	12.5
Often	8.7	6.6	9.7
Very often	10.3	6.8	12.8

Own Alcohol and Drug Use

Nearly 80% of the sample seldom or never used alcohol or drugs while 12.2% sometimes used alcohol or drugs. Only 9% used drugs or alcohol often or very often. Happy and unhappy couples also differed in their own alcohol and drug use. Over 88% of the happy couples seldom or never used alcohol or drugs compared with about 72% of unhappy couples. About 7% of the happy couples sometimes used alcohol or drugs while over 15% of the unhappy couples sometimes used alcohol or drugs. Only 4.2% of happy couples used alcohol or drugs often or very often while 12.4% of the unhappy couples often or very often used alcohol or drugs.

OWN DRUG USE	TOTAL SAMPLE	HAPPY MARRIAGES	UNHAPPY MARRIAGES
Never	65.2%	77.1%	57.6%
Seldom	13.8	11.3	14.9
Sometimes	12.2	7.5	15.2
Often	4.8	2.3	6.6
Very often	4.1	1.9	5.8

Abuse Between Parents

For the total sample, over 60% of the couples reported that abuse seldom or never occurred between parents, and about one-fifth (20.4%) reported that it sometimes occurred. Over 18.6% of couples reported that abuse occurred often or very often between parents.

The unhappy couples had more reports of seeing abuse between their parents than did the happy couples. Unhappy couples witnessed more abuse between their parents, with over 24% reporting that it occurred often or very often compared with only 9.4% of happy couples. Over 22% of unhappy couples and 16% of happy couples reported that abuse sometimes occurred between their parents. Abuse between parents never or seldom occurred in the families of 74% of happy couples and 53.4% of unhappy couples.

ABUSE BETWEEN PARENTS	TOTAL SAMPLE	HAPPY MARRIAGES	UNHAPPY MARRIAGES
Never	43.2%	57.1%	35.8%
Seldom	17.8	17.1	17.7
Sometimes	20.4	16.4	22.3
Often or very often	18.6	9.4	24.3

Abused by Parents

In terms of being abused by parents, 72% of the total sample reported that they were seldom or never abused by parents and 15.6% reported that they were sometimes abused by parents. Only 12.3% of couples reported being abused often or very often by parents. When comparing happy and unhappy couples, 5.4% of happy couples experienced abuse often or very often while 17% of unhappy couples experienced abuse often or very often. Eleven percent of happy couples and 19% of unhappy couples sometimes experienced abuse by parents. About 84% of happy couples and 64% of unhappy couples seldom or never experienced abuse by parents.

ABUSED BY PARENTS	TOTAL SAMPLE	HAPPY MARRIAGES	UNHAPPY MARRIAGES
Never	56.7%	71.5%	47.8%
Seldom	15.3	12.3	16.6
Sometimes	15.6	11.0	18.7
Often or very often	12.3	5.4	17.0

Abuse by Anyone

Of the entire sample, 68% of the couples were seldom or never abused by anyone and 21.5% were sometimes abused by someone. About 10% were often or very often abused by someone.

For happy couples, 7.4% experienced abuse often or very often by someone while 13% of unhappy couples experienced abuse often or very often by someone. Thirteen percent of happy couples were sometimes abused by someone while twice as many unhappy couples (27%) were sometimes abused by someone. In addition, over 79% of happy couples were seldom or never abused by anyone, while 60.3% of unhappy couples were seldom or never abused by anyone.

ABUSED BY ANYONE	TOTAL SAMPLE	HAPPY MARRIAGES	UNHAPPY MARRIAGES
Never	39.5%	56.7%	29.3%
Seldom	28.5	22.8	31.0
Sometimes	21.5	13.2	27.0
Often or very often	10.5	7.4	12.9

Abused by Partner

In terms of the total sample, over 74% were seldom or never abused by their partner while 17.5% were sometimes abused by their partner. Over 8.5% were abused often or very often by their partner.

One percent of the happy couples experienced abuse often or very often by their partner while over 14% of unhappy couples experienced abuse often or very often by their partner. A small percentage of happy couples (2.8%) were sometimes abused by their partner while a much larger percentage of unhappy couples were sometimes abused by their partner (27.6%). The greatest discrepancy between happy and unhappy couples involved the number that were seldom or never abused by their partner. Over 96% of happy couples were seldom or never abused by their partner while 58.3% of unhappy couples were seldom or never abused by their partner.

Abused by Partner	Total Sample	Happy Marriages	Unhappy Marriages
Never	55.2%	87.0%	34.9%
Seldom	19.0	9.1	23.4
Sometimes	17.5	2.8	27.6
Often or very often	8.5	1.1	14.3

Preparing for Marriage or Enriching Your Marriage

Overview of the PREPARE/ENRICH Program

The *PREPARE Program* is for premarital couples and the *ENRICH Program* is for married couples. The PREPARE/ENRICH Program is one of most popular and scientifically developed programs to help couples strengthen their relationship.

The program has been taken by over 1,000,000 couples in the United States over the last 10 years. The program was developed at the University of Minnesota over 20 years ago by Dr. David Olson, Dr. David Fournier and Dr. Joan Druckman. The program is offered by over 45,000 professional counselors and clergy of all denominations in all 50 states and in over ten other countries (Australia, Canada, England, Germany, Hong Kong, Japan, Korea, Singapore, South Africa, Sweden, and Taiwan).

The overall goal of the PREPARE/ENRICH Program is to help you to build your strengths as a couple. This is done primarily by providing you with insights into your relationship and teaching you relationship skills (particularly communication and conflict resolution skills) that you can use to help make your relationship grow and develop. The program helps you to identify your couple strengths and growth areas. By resolving your issues (growth areas), you can also turn them into strengths.

The first step in the PREPARE/ENRICH Program is to locate a professional trained to offer the program. We will describe later how to locate a trained professional, which includes professional counselors and clergy of all denominations. The typical number of sessions ranges from 4-6 depending on the counselor's approach and your needs and desires as a couple.

Next, you and your partner would each take a couple questionnaire called PREPARE or ENRICH that asks questions about 20 important areas of your couple relationship including communication, conflict resolution, roles, personality, family and friends and other relevant issues. Your responses are computer scored and the professional you meet with will receive a 15 page computer report about your relationship.

Six Couple Exercises in Program

As part of the feedback process with the counselor, you will complete six couples exercises using a 25 page workbook called *Building A Strong Marriage*. The six couple exercises are designed to achieve the following goals:

1. To identify your couple strengths and potential growth areas.
2. To help you build your communication skills, including assertiveness and active listening.
3. To develop your skills in resolving couple conflict using a Ten Step Model of Conflict Resolution.
4. To explore your family of origin and your couple relationship.
5. To help you develop a financial budget and discuss your short and long term financial plans.
6. To explore and discuss personal goals, couple goals and family goals and develop an action plan using the CHANGE Model.

In the next section entitled **"Experiencing the PREPARE Program,"** a couple who went through the PREPARE Program describe their experiences. Over 95% of the couples who have taken the program highly recommend it to others.

To Find a Professional Offering the PREPARE/ENRICH Program in Your Area

To locate a trained professional who offers the program in your area, you can visit our web site at: **www.lifeinnovation.com.** At the web site, look under "For Couples," click on the section "Locating a PREPARE/ENRICH Counselor." Enter your zip code and it will produce a list of trained professionals you can contact for more information or an appointment.

The web site also provides more information about the PREPARE/ENRICH Program and studies on the value of usefulness of the program. You can also take a short Couple Quiz and get feedback individually or as a couple on the web site.

You can also contact us at: *Life Innovations, Inc., P.O. Box 190, Minneapolis, MN 55440-0190, toll free: (800) 331-1661, fax: (651) 636-1668.*

Experiencing the PREPARE Program
by Luke Knutson

"You two went to counseling!" my friend said. *"Why in the world would you guys need to go see a counselor?"* *"Well, that was exactly my reaction when my fiancee first brought it up two months ago,"* I responded. I asked her why we would need to go to counseling if we don't have any problems in our relationship. I didn't really see a need to go. I thought it would just be a waste of time and energy. But Julie wouldn't let the issue drop so I decided to be open-minded about it. The more I thought about it, the less apprehensive I became. Julie had been surfing the web looking for information on premarital counseling and came across a program called PREPARE. She had also recalled that a couple we knew had been through this program before they were married a couple years ago.

Julie showed me the PREPARE website and asked if I would read through it to see what I thought of it. I read through the information about PREPARE and found out that it was a very well known premarital counseling program and has been taken by over 1 million couples. The site also explained that PREPARE was a questionnaire designed to measure a couple's strength and growth areas.

I told Julie that I was very skeptical of tests like this and that I was questioning how accurate or helpful the results of the questionnaire would be. When I said that, Julie gave me this look that conveyed both disappointment and anger and at that moment I knew what I had to do.

Once we both agreed that we would go to premarital counseling, we went to the **www.lifeinnovations.com** website and clicked on *"Find a PREPARE/ENRICH counselor."* Then we entered our zip code and entered the type of counselor we wanted and pressed *"Search."* A few moments later a list came up on the screen with about twenty different counselors, and their phone numbers. We picked a counselor from the list and called to set up our first session.

Taking the PREPARE Couple Inventory

The day of the first counseling session Julie and I were both a little nervous. We didn't know exactly what to expect since we had never been to counseling or met this counselor before. But after we arrived and met and talked with him a little bit, we felt more at ease. After we talked for a little while he handed each of us a PREPARE answer sheet and question booklet to fill out separately. I still felt anxious and it was like I was taking an exam in school or something. But I tried to remember what our counselor said about not viewing it as a test and that there are no right or wrong answers. As I went through the questions I would sometimes come across one that brought up an issue that Julie and I had never really talked about before like financial issues or how we're going to raise our children. Overall, I would say it was actually kind of fun to fill out and to think about all of the different issues it touched on. On the way home in the car after taking PREPARE, Julie and I started asking each other how we answered certain questions. Sometimes we responded the same way, and on a few questions we answered differently. On the questions where we disagreed we discussed our reasoning behind our answers and tried to explain to the other why we answered the way we did. It was already becoming clear to me that the PREPARE Program was going to be good for us.

Discussing Our Strengths and Growth Areas

We went back for our first feedback session a couple weeks later and we were both anxious to see the results of the inventory. The counselor began the session by asking us about our experience taking the inventory. Then he informed us that the goal of the first exercise was to increase our awareness of Strength and Growth Areas in our relationship. For the first part of the exercise he gave both Julie and I a list of the eleven areas that are included in PREPARE and had us mark three areas that we thought were strengths in our relationship and three areas that we thought needed some improvement.

I chose marriage expectations, leisure activities, and communication for relationship strengths and conflict resolution, financial management, and spiritual beliefs for growth areas. The counselor had each of us take turns telling which areas we picked as strengths. After one of us would read a Strength he would then look at the computer report and tell us if we had chosen correctly. He would bring up areas where we did actually agree and then pick out some individual questions that we disagreed on.

I was surprised by Julie's reaction after I revealed my third Relationship Strength. I said, *"I think another one of our strengths is communication. I think we communicate really well and we are good at expressing our feelings with one another."* Immediately after I mentioned what I thought was our third relationship strength, communication, I heard this scoff come from Julie. She said, *"What are you talking about? I put Communication as one of our Growth Areas!"* So we went off on a tangent about why we thought communication was a strength or a growth area.

During this discussion, our counselor talked about how men and women differ in their communication styles and that may be why we differed on whether it was a strength or growth area in our relationship. After covering all of our Strength Areas (or Growth Areas depending on who you ask) we went on to discuss our Growth Areas.

We went through the same process with our Growth Areas but discussed them in greater length. We spent some time delving into each Growth Area by discussing the items and trying to come up with things we could do differently in order to try and strengthen these areas. Although there was some tension when talking about some of these issues, overall I think this exercise was really helpful for our relationship.

Improving Our Communication Skills

The second exercise stressed the importance of good communication skills, specifically, assertiveness and active listening. Julie and I had each completed the homework that our counselor had assigned to us the previous session. For the homework, we had to make a Wish List of three things we would like our partner to do more often. But before we discussed our lists the counselor described the meaning of assertiveness and active listening and then asked us to assess ourselves and each other in this area.

I said I thought I was pretty high in assertiveness and that my active listening skills were pretty good as well. Julie said that her active listening was pretty high but that her assertiveness might be a little low. I agreed with Julie in her self-assessment but she didn't exactly agree with mine. She thought my listening skills were lacking. She said, *"I think you're active listening skills need a little work, and in fact, that was one of the things on my wish list."* After hearing this, the counselor decided to let Julie start with the first item on her Wish List.

She said, *"I wish you would listen to me more. I feel like sometimes when I'm talking to you, you just tune me out. It feels like some of the things I say go in one ear and right out the other."* She also pointed out that it usually happens when I'm watching TV or listening to the radio. After she was finished, I tried to repeat back what I heard her say, and she said that I paraphrased her statements pretty well. We discussed this issue and then went through the rest of our Wish Lists the same way and a lot of important issues were raised that neither of us had really mentioned before.

I think we both found it easier to bring up things we would like our partner to do more often in the company of a neutral third party. Our counselor did a good job facilitating our discussion and helped make it a constructive and less confrontational atmosphere than if we were to have brought these issues up on our own.

Improving Our Conflict Resolution Skills

The third exercise was called *"Ten Steps to Resolving Couple Conflict."* The counselor explained to us that this was an exercise designed to help identify conflicts that need to be discussed. He also said that it provides a series of specific steps to go through in order to help us work toward a solution. We decided to work on a problem that we've been noticing more and more lately. The problem has to do with how we interact with each other during the week. When Julie and I get together after work, whether it be at my apartment or hers, we tend to want to do things differently. I like to come home, change into comfortable clothes, sit on the couch, watch TV and unwind for a while. Julie, on the other hand, likes to come home, immediately tell me everything that happened that day at work, and then start working again, doing things like cleaning, paying the bills, and running errands. Sometimes she says things like, *"Why are you so lazy?"* and *"I feel like you'd rather watch TV than hear about my day."* And in response, I say, *"Why don't you just relax for a little bit, instead of running around the house?"* So basically, I like to relax first and then talk and get things done after I've unwound, and she likes to talk and get things done immediately after she gets home, and then relax later that night.

Over the course of the counseling session we discussed the problem, talked about how we each contribute to the problem, and what we've tried in the past that hasn't worked. After brainstorming for a while, we came up with a solution we both agreed on, and decided to work together to see if this solution would work. We also agreed to meet with each other after a few weeks to discuss our progress and reward each other for contributing to a solution.

Exploring Our Family of Origins

For the next exercise, the counselor facilitated a discussion about our couple relationship and how it relates to our families of origin. He also showed us the *Couple and Family Map* and what it represented.

Julie and I already knew that our families-of-origin were different in some respects. My family was pretty flexible growing up and her family was a little more strict. My family talked openly, often discussing disagreements and conflicts, while Julie's family talked openly about some things but tended to avoid arguments and conflict altogether. We talked about our families and how they compared with our couple relationship and then our counselor showed us the Couple and Family Map. The map illustrated some of the same things we had talked about earlier and it was interesting to see it plotted on the map.

After reviewing the map, the counselor asked us to think of things from our family-of-origin that we want to bring into our marriage and also things that we do not want to bring into the marriage. I guess we didn't really realize how influential our families-of-origin were on the way we interacted as a couple. Hopefully we will be able to build on the positive things we have learned from our families-of-origin and avoid some of the negative qualities that our families might've had as well.

Dealing with Our Finances

For the next session, our counselor had Julie and I complete a budget worksheet. It took us about half an hour to fill in our earnings and expenses and then list our short and long term financial goals. At the next counseling session, we started by discussing what we had learned from the budget exercise. I immediately said, *"We learned that Julie likes to spend money and I like to save money."* Julie responded by saying, *"I learned that he's a cheapskate and I'm not."* We went on to discuss how Julie and I differ in our spending habits and how that is sometimes a source of conflict in our relationship. Our counselor brought up some of the questions on PREPARE that were disagreement and special focus items and we talked through some of those issues as well. We also brought up some of our ideas about our short and long term financial goals. Overall, both Julie and I thought that the budget exercise was beneficial because we had never really developed a budget before. It also brought up some important issues that we need to discuss further.

Focusing on Our Personal, Couple, and Family Goals

For the last couple exercise, we had to write down our personal, couple, and family goals. The counselor had us take turns sharing with each other our list of goals. He also helped point out the differences and similarities between our lists and facilitated the discussion about how we were going to reach these goals. Then we went over the CHANGE Model and the counselor explained what it was and how we could use it to achieve our goals. We picked a goal that we both agreed on and decided to use the CHANGE Model to see if it would help us to accomplish our goal. We also decided that our reward, if we accomplished the goal, would be to rent a cabin up north for a nice relaxing weekend alone.

My Final Reaction

In retrospect, I'm really glad my fiancee convinced me to go to counseling and experience the PREPARE Program. I was a little apprehensive when she first told me about the program because I did not think anything was wrong with our relationship. But, now that I've gone through the program, I've come to the realization that counseling isn't necessarily just for people who have problems or major issues to overcome. It can also be used by couples like us, who have a strong relationship with relatively few issues, to provide a way to build on our strengths and grow as a couple.

If You Have Ongoing Relationship Problems

If you have many ongoing issues in your couple relationship that are not getting resolved, it is important to seek professional help. The sooner you get help, the sooner and more likely it is that these issues can turn around from stumbling blocks to stepping stones. When problems are not worked through, they tend to destroy the core of the relationship and weaken it dramatically.

While this book might provide you and your partner with many helpful ideas, if you have tried them and your problems still persist, you then need to seek professional help.

One way for you to evaluate and rebuild your relationship is to take the ENRICH Program. The ENRICH Program will give you a comprehensive evaluation of your couple strengths as well as what specific areas in your relationship are problematic. The ENRICH questionnaire will be administered by a professional who is trained to use and interpret the inventory. You will also complete the six couple exercises identified previously.

To find a counselor or clergy in your area trained to administer ENRICH, visit the Life Innovations web site at **lifeinnovations.com** and on the section called, "For Couples," click on "Find a P/E Counselor." You may do a search by using your zip code or the state in which you live, as well as if you have a preference for a clergy or a professional counselor.

Another option is to select a licensed marriage counselor (also called a marital/couple therapist) from the Yellow Pages of your phone company. You should look for counselors that are licensed in your state as a *"Marital and Family Therapist."* You can call the state licensing board for marital and family therapy for a list of licensed professionals in your area.

When you contact a professional counselor, ask them the following questions:

Are you licensed as a marriage and family therapist in your state?

If not, what training have you had to work with couples?

How much success have you had working with couples?

What type of couple assessment do you use?

How many sessions do you usually recommend?

What are your charges and is there a sliding scale?

Will my insurance cover any expenses?

Do you want to mainly see us together as a couple?

If you feel comfortable with the counselor's answers to these and other questions you may have, then set up an appointment. Remember that finding the counselor who is right for you and your partner is a very personal decision. The therapy experience can be very different depending on how you and your therapist interact.

Another excellent source to find a qualified marital therapist is by calling the *American Association for Marital and Family Therapy* (AAMFT) in Washington, D.C. at (202) 452-0109 or visit their web site at **www.aamft.org.**

About the Authors

David H. Olson, Ph.D.

Professor, Family Social Science, University of Minnesota and President of Life Innovations. He is past President of the *National Council on Family Relations* (NCFR) and the *Upper Midwest Association of Marital and Family Therapy* (UMMFT). He is a Fellow and clinical member of the *American Psychological Association* (APA) and the *American Association for Marital & Family Therapy* (AAMFT).

He has received several awards from national organizations (AAMFT, AFTA, ACA, ACME and Penn State University) for his theoretical, research and programs for couples and families. He is best known for his work on the Circumplex Model (Couple and Family Map) and the PREPARE/ENRICH Program for couples.

He has published 100 journal articles and over 20 books including: *Marriage & Family—Diversity & Strengths* (2000) and *Building Relationships* (1999).

He shares his life with an extraordinary woman, Karen and they have three fantastic children (Hans, Chris and Amy) and five fun loving grandchildren (Adrienne, Evan, Chelsea, Alex, and Ava).

Amy K. Olson-Sigg, B.A.

Research Associate at Life Innovations, Minneapolis, Minnesota. She has her degree in Family Studies and Psychology from Concordia College in St. Paul. She has co-authored several articles on the PREPARE/ENRICH Program and co-authored the book *Building Relationships: Developing Skills for Life* (1999). She served as a student representative on the Board of Directors of the Minnesota Council on Family Relations (MCFR).

She is extremely grateful for her beautiful family of origin and her dazzling family of procreation: husband Daniel, daughters Adrienne and Ava and son Evan.

Share Your Story to Inspire Others

A premise of this book is that other's knowledge and experience can become our own, and we would like to publish your story in an upcoming book.

Please send us your personal story to inspire and/or inform other couples. These stories can be about overcoming relationship obstacles, simple things that you have learned along the way in your relationship. You may want to share principles or ideas from this book that enhanced your couple relationship.

Be sure to include your name, return address, business or home phone, fax, and email address. We will contact you for final permission before using your story.

Send to:
Amy Olson
Life Innovations, Inc.
P.O. Box 190
Minneapolis, MN 55440-0190

Fax: 651-636-1668
Email: cs@lifeinnovation.com

We look forward to hearing from you!